If Gargoyles Could Talk

If Gargoyles Could Talk

Sketches of Duke University

William E. King

CAROLINA ACADEMIC PRESS

Durham, North Carolina

Paperback ISBN 978-1-5310-1692-0
ISBN 0-89089-814-6
LCCN 97-75079

CAROLINA ACADEMIC PRESS
700 Kent Street
Durham, North Carolina 27701
Telephone (919) 489-7486
Fax (919) 493-5668
www.cap-press.com

Photographic Credits

All photographs courtesy of Duke University Archives, except:

    page 43, Library of Congress, LC-USZ62-12145;
    page 52, Duke University Special Collections Library;
    page 89, Musee des Troia Guerres;
    pages 158 and 171, Les Todd;
    page 159, Duke University Photography;
    page 182, Bruce Feeley.

2019 Printing

Printed in the United States of America

This book is dedicated to
H. B. K., C. H. K., and J. E. K.
who have shared many Duke experiences

Contents

Foreword

Twenty-five years ago the diligent efforts of a number of people connected with Duke University paid off in the establishment of the University Archives. For many years William B. Hamilton, professor of history and feisty leader in many good university causes, Benjamin E. Powell, university librarian, and Mattie U. Russell, director of the library's Manuscript Department, had pushed hard for the creation of a separate archives, where important historic materials concerning the university could be safely and centrally stored as well as properly catalogued and made available for research and reference.

With President Terry Sanford's blessings and financial assistance and the enthusiastic support of trustee and alumnus, W. M. Upchurch, the Archives was established in 1972 and Duke was also fortunate in the appointment of the first University Archivist, William E. King. A Duke undergraduate with a Ph.D. in History from Duke, King also had the additional blessing of having parents who were both Duke alumni. His professional training as a historian complemented nicely the love for the institution that ran deep in his family.

This is not the place to recount the many ways in which the university has benefited from the existence of the Archives. Many of us wonder, in fact, how the university managed without them for so long.

One of the unanticipated benefits of the Archives has been the series of articles concerning Trinity College and Duke history that King began to write in 1990. Appearing in the weekly campus publication, *Dialogue,* the seventy-one essays have covered a wide variety of topics in a fascinating and easily digested form.

Chronologically, six of the pieces deal with the years from 1838 until 1892, when first Union Institute and then Trinity College were in Randolph County, some seventy-five miles west of where the institution is now located. Twenty-two articles relate to the period from 1892 down to late 1924, when Trinity College was in Durham and began its steady climb toward academic strength. Thirty essays deal with Duke University since 1924, and twelve are sufficiently general to defy periodization.

Topically, the articles run the gamut from leading personalities in the institution's past to the construction of well-loved buildings. Athletics as well as individual professional schools receive attention. An almost-forgotten president; the origin of the Blue Devil mascot; the stonemasons and setters who helped erect the Tudor Gothic buildings on West Campus; the student dance bands of the 1930s;

the employment of distinguished Jewish scholars who fled Nazi Germany; the controversy over tobacco through the years—all these and more are illuminated by King's carefully researched and engagingly written articles.

Bringing them together so that a wider audience among those who love or are interested in Duke may enjoy them was a capital idea.

Robert F. Durden
Professor Emeritus of History
Duke University
August, 1997

Introduction

This volume reproduces a series of articles from the *Dialogue,* a weekly campus newspaper published by the Duke News Service. In 1990, Geoffrey Mock, the editor, asked me to contribute periodic articles on Duke history. As such, the topics are wide-ranging, often determined by issues of the moment or in response to frequently asked questions. They are not inclusive of the history of the university, having obvious omissions of subject matter. With seventy-one articles in print, Gerry Eidenier, Director of the Gothic Books Program, encouraged me to compile them in a book to share with a larger audience.

Despite the variety of topics, there are some evident themes in the compilation. Foremost is the fact that Duke University is founded upon its predecessor institutions, Union Institute, Normal College and Trinity College. The school has had multiple name changes, a relocation from Randolph County to Durham, and a significant expansion of its original Durham campus at the time of transition from a college to a university. But as the Board of Trustees noted in December, 1924 when the institution officially became Duke University: "Through all this outward change it has kept one soul; it has been guided by the same controlling faiths. Now it changes again to meet changing conditions." Though radically different from its beginning, Duke University is built upon Trinity College, especially the Durham experience since 1892, but also the 19th century experience in Randolph County since 1838–39.

Duke University's history can be confusing. For example, the institution marked its 100th anniversary with an elaborate yearlong celebration in 1938–39 and its 50th anniversary in 1974–75. It has been an academy, a college with a primary focus of training teachers and preachers, a liberal arts college and a multifaceted research university. All too often it is tempting, when writing or speaking about the university, to ignore its complexity and overlook historical perspective. It is fervently hoped that these articles of selected subjects will add clarity, correct error, and illustrate the varied contributions of the many individuals who have made Duke University what it is today. I have attempted to include new information, discovered in the daily operation of the University Archives, in each article in hopes that it will enrich and aid in understanding.

This book is not an authorized, official study. The selection of topics, interpretation and errors are mine alone. It is, however, written with a demonstrated loyalty to Duke University. I do not know when my first visit to campus occurred but it was most probably at an early age when my mother served as president of the alumnae association. With a father, Carl H. King, who was a graduate of the last class of Trinity College in 1924 and mother, Mary Elizabeth Eskridge, who was a graduate of the first class of Duke University in 1925, and with three earned degrees from Duke myself as well as having additional Duke degrees among my brother, wife and children, it is no wonder Duke blue and white are my favorite colors. However, I hope my education in the history department is demonstrated by well-researched, professional articles.

Numerous individuals have been of assistance in many ways. Geoffrey Mock edited the initial articles. The staff of the University Archives, Thomas F. Harkins, Daniel L. Daily, and Robert Todd Crumley, suggested topics and assisted with research. Doris C. Parrish, Peggy W. Satterfield and Carol E. Walter prepared the manuscripts. I also am indebted to whose who wrote letters of encouragement since it has not always been easy making deadlines while meeting the responsibilities of the archival program. Helen King has been especially encouraging throughout the endeavor. Funds from the Isobel Craven Drill Endowment for the University Archives assisted in the preparation of the manuscript. In the spirit of the cooperative endeavor that these articles have been, any proceeds from this book will be added to an archival endowment fund or a university scholarship fund.

William E. King
Duke University Archives
July 30, 1997

If Gargoyles Could Talk

Brantley York:
The Leader With a Calling

Duke University dates its origin as an educational institution from 1838. Not unlike most schools, it has had numerous name changes as well as a major geographic relocation during its history. For obvious reasons one can be confused about Duke's history. For example, the University Archives has programs on file for the celebration of a one hundredth anniversary in 1938–39 and a fiftieth anniversary in 1974–75! To further compound the issue there is another date for the centennial observance of the opening of Trinity College in Durham. No wonder that upon accepting the provisions of James B. Duke's Indenture of Trust in 1924 the Board of Trustees noted "the institution changes again to meet changing conditions."

The individual who founded the school and set it on its course was Brantley York, a noted nineteenth-century educator, preacher, lecturer, and author. The setting was the fertile rolling hill country of piedmont North Carolina in northwest Randolph County approximately seventy-five miles west of Durham. By the 1830s farmers in this area were beginning to experience prosperity through developing markets in eastern North Carolina and in South Carolina. Populated by a growing middle class of hard-working, devout Methodists and Quakers, the leading families greatly desired schooling for their children.

In the manner of the day there were isolated one-room schoolhouses used occasionally when a teacher might appear much like the traveling ordained circuit riders that represented organized religion. Sometime in the early 1830s one farmer, John Brown, built such a school that was used intermittently. By 1838 community leaders sought a teacher who would locate permanently and provide continuous education.

From nearby Bush Creek, Brantley York was one of their own. Captivated by the excitement of learning, York was largely self-taught having attended school only thirteen months in a ten-year period. Yet by age nineteen, he was reading one thousand pages a week through the lending library of Ebenezer Methodist

Brantley York (1805–1891), founder and principal of Union Institute, made a career of founding schools, publishing textbooks and lecturing on temperance.

Church. At the time he was contacted about teaching at Brown's Schoolhouse, York was seeking ordination as a Methodist minister. He began teaching in the spring of 1838. The need was correctly perceived for the school had to be moved into a new building by August. With sixty-nine students, York also had to have an assistant as well. By February, 1839 York engineered the organization of an educational society to provide governance and financial support. Yet another building was built, this time to be called Union Institute, so named not for patriotic reasons but because of the uniting of Methodist and Quaker interests in education. Incorporated as an academy in 1841, the school later became Normal College in 1851, Trinity College in 1859 and after removal to Durham in 1892, Duke University in 1924. The University selected 1838 as its origin because from that date there has been an uninterrupted progression of educational growth and service.

Despite blindness that developed by age forty-eight, York had discovered his calling as a founder of schools. After leaving Union Institute in 1842, he founded six more schools in five counties. He also published a popular series of English grammars plus a book of practical applied arithmetic and legal forms. He was a popular revival preacher and temperance lecturer as well. Late in life, before his death at age eighty-six, York estimated that he had preached or lectured over 8,000 times and taught more than 15,000 students.

In an interesting coincidence, sentiments stated in the preamble to the Union Institute Society and James B. Duke's Indenture of Trust are quite similar. Written in 1839 by Brantley York, those joining to provide educational opportunity in Randolph County did so "...possessing no small share of philanthropy and patriotism, and believing that ignorance and error were not only the bane of religions but also of civil society." Without knowledge of the Society's statement, the Duke Indenture expressed the same idea in stating that "education...is next to religion, the greatest civilizing influence." "Education," "religion," and concern for "civil society" are words in harmony although expressed eighty-five years apart. While "changing to meet changing conditions" is a hallmark of the institution, "guidance by the same controlling faiths" is not uncommon either.

____ Duke's Humble Beginning As Union Institute

"Union Institute," the catalogue reads, "is eighteen miles southwest of Greensboro in the hill country between the Uwharrie and Deep rivers; as nearly as any place, exempt from disease, and in the midst of a moral and intelligent community." This appeal was for boarding students at the institution which has evolved into Duke University. Founders' Day honors over 150 years of history beginning in the spring of 1838 when Brantley York, a local preacher and teacher, began instruction at a school which has continued uninterrupted, although under different names and in different locations.

In northwest rural Randolph County, about seventy-five miles west of Durham, hard-working and God-fearing Methodist and Quaker families desired a permanent school for their children. York began teaching in a one-room log school called Brown's Schoolhouse, but demand quickly necessitated a move into a new log building and then into a frame two-room building on three acres of land. The instant success faltered as the Quaker students gravitated to their own nearby school, now Guilford College, and as the girls were attracted to a nearby Methodist school exclusively for women, now known as Greensboro College. To counter those losses and assist York, who was working exceedingly hard and also going blind, Irene Leach and later Braxton Craven were employed as teaching assistants. Craven succeeded York as principal of the school in 1842 and he and Irene Leach were married in 1844. For forty years until his death in 1882, the history of the school as Union Institute academy and then as Normal College and Trinity College is largely the biography of Braxton Craven.

The original site of Union Institute and Trinity College was in Trinity in Randolph County, seventy-five miles west of Durham.

Union Institute was part of the growth of academies in nineteenth century educational history. In 1830 nearly 1,000 academies were scattered throughout the country. By 1850 New England alone had about 1,000 academies, and the southern states had approximately 2,700. Academies were more prevalent in the south where public schools supported by taxation developed slowly. However, individual academies had a precarious history. In the rural south they were dependent upon successful farming for economic support and those that succeeded did so usually by developing a special constituency due to affiliation with a religious body or by the personality and reputation of its leader.

Between 1843 and 1850 enrollment at Union Institute averaged 105 students but it varied from a low of 28 to a high of 184. A community grew up around the school as people moved to the vicinity to educate their children. The principal sources of income were farming and boarding of students. The school term consisted of two, twenty-two-week sessions usually spaced to permit help with spring planting. Students could find room and board and have their clothes washed for $5.00 a month but they had to provide their own candles for study.

Instruction was organized into five academic departments: English, mathematics, natural science, Latin, and Greek. English, mathematics, and Latin spread their curriculum over four years. Natural science and Greek were offered only after the first year. Instruction consisted of reading and recitation from selected textbooks in progressively difficult subjects. For example, in mathematics one began studying arithmetic and progressed through algebra, geometry, trigonometry, surveying, mechanics, architecture, optics, and mathematical astronomy. The department of English began with spelling and pronunciation, grammar, geography, and ancient history, and progressed through bookkeeping, poetry, rhetoric, logic, mental and moral philosophy, and political economy. The curriculum was designed to "properly develop and discipline the mind" and prepare one for college should one have the time and opportunity.

Tuition varied from $5.00 to $10.00 per session depending upon the department and level of instruction. Typical costs were $30.00 per session for room, board and tuition. In good years the academy could average $1,200 gross income per year with an average expenditure of $224 for "help for indigent young men" or scholarships.

Out-of-class activities centered around Sabbath School and worship services for, as the catalogue stated, "morals are cultivated as well as minds." The single student organization was the Columbian Literary Society which promoted interest in public speaking and debate, conducted literary discussions, and invited lecturers to campus.

Despite the initial changes in leadership and withdrawal of patronage, Union Institute succeeded as an academy largely because of the popularity of Braxton Craven as a teacher, preacher, writer, and public lecturer. It became a well-known institution attracting students from throughout North Carolina as well as from Virginia and South Carolina and even far-away Missouri. Craven, nevertheless, believed the school had reached its maximum growth as an academy and as the decade of the 1850s began he made plans to develop it into a college.

‗ Braxton Craven: The Longest-Serving President

In educational history one frequently used to hear that every institution is but the lengthened shadow of one person. Such a sentiment accurately reflects the nineteenth-century history of Trinity College. For forty years one man, Braxton Craven, presided over the institution giving it a special identity that ultimately led to university status in another place at another time.

Braxton Craven was born in 1822 in rural Randolph County on the North Carolina frontier where all too often hard work had to be accompanied by luck for one to overcome imposing obstacles. At age seven he was living with an adoptive Quaker family where constant physical labor was expected in exchange for room and board. He later reported he was "sorely oppressed" as a youth but he also learned industry, thrift, and self-reliance. Converted at a nearby Methodist Church, he seized upon religion and education as a means for personal betterment. Almost exclusively self-taught, he gained influence in the community by teaching school and preaching at Sunday schools whenever the ever-present demands of planting and harvesting permitted. After saving some money, Craven enrolled in the nearby Quaker school, now Guilford College, when it admitted non-Quakers for the first time. When his savings ran out after two years he returned to his home community to assist Brantley York who had recently organized a growing school. The school was known as Union Institute because of the uniting of Methodist and Quaker family interests in providing permanent education for their children. In 1842 Craven succeeded York as principal when York was called to organize another school. For the next four decades, the history of the school was largely the biography of Braxton Craven.

After conducting a successful academy for nine years, Craven had the institution chartered by the legislature as Normal College with its graduates licensed to teach by the state. Ever aware of the need for consistent income, he simultaneously sought support from the Methodist Church promising to educate preministerial students free of charge. Church ties proved stronger and in 1859 Craven changed the name of the school again, this time to Trinity College. As the college outgrew the boarding capacity of the community,

Braxton Craven (1822–1882) carried a full teaching load throughout his presidency.

ambitious plans were approved for an expanded all-purpose building which included the school's first dormitory. Civil War, however, halted expansion and almost ended the school. Without Craven's commitment and personality it is doubtful that Trinity College would have survived the poverty of the defeated South.

Before his death in 1882, Braxton Craven presided over a single institution with three different names, with a faculty that grew from two to seven to ten members, and with an enrollment that fluctuated from less than twenty to over two hundred students. Craven himself taught Ancient Languages, Mental and Moral Science, Metaphysics, Rhetoric and Logic, National and Constitutional Law, and Biblical Literature. At the same time he constantly preached and lectured throughout the region, wrote two novels, and engaged the Smithsonian Institution in debate over the exact time for the eclipse of the sun. When his calculations proved to be correct the Smithsonian sought his services but he politely declined. Aware of his lack of an earned degree he acquired permission to stand examination upon the entire course of study at Randolph Macon College in Virginia. When he passed all exams without ever attending any classes, that college awarded him an honorary A.B. degree. Later the Universities of North Carolina and Missouri, among others, awarded him honorary degrees in recognition of his contributions to fostering higher education.

Though a strict disciplinarian and formal in the pulpit and classroom, Craven was at ease in an educational setting. He always boarded students in his home. The terms of his will reveal strong family ties as well as a lifestyle that undoubtedly contributed to his popularity among generations of students. After providing for his wife and assuring that his children "be thoroughly educated," he bequeathed modest but prized possessions as follows: to his wife, Irene, the mantel clock and his melodeon; to daughters Emma and Kate, the piano and gray mare named Bounce, and the silver pitcher and goblet; and to sons James and Willie, the young black horse named Jeff, and his gold watch.

Craven's legacy is a school that survived and even prospered in the face of tremendous odds. He personally selected the name Trinity College and the motto, "Eruditio et Religio," that defines the character of Duke University today. We honor him with the name of Craven Quadrangle and through the awarding of the Braxton Craven Scholarship. Numerous descendants have graduated from Duke University and three have served with distinction on the Board of Trustees—James B. Craven, grandson; J. Braxton Craven, Jr., great-grandson; and Isobel Craven Drill, great-granddaughter. In 1989 Mrs. Drill received the university's Distinguished Alumni Award, the highest award of the General Alumni Association. Active participation in the affairs of the institution by one family for over 150 years is a worthy tradition.

Forward-Thinking President Craven
Starts Alumni Association

In over one hundred and fifty years Duke University has had two locations and five name changes but one of its oldest, most constant components has been an Alumni Association. Founded in 1838 as Union Institute academy, the school became a degree-granting college upon authorization of the legislature of North Carolina in 1852. At Commencement weekend in 1858 with the college not a decade old and the entire number of graduates totaling forty-one, President Braxton Craven called for the creation of an Alumni Association. The president's call was met with considerable debate for it took three meetings, one of which convened at 7:00 a.m., before a constitution was signed by fifteen members on June 23, 1858. Lemuel Johnson, who with his brother constituted the entire graduating class of 1853, was elected the first president, and C. C. Cole, '54, became the first secretary. Johnson, then a professor, taught mathematics at the college for twenty-six years and Cole, then an editor of the *Greensboro Times* had a promising career cut short by his death in the battle of Chancellorsville in the Civil War.

In the language of the day the objects of the Alumni Association were "to keep green in our memories the pleasures of college life; to promote and sustain refined and extended scholarship; to encourage a higher degree of morals among literary men; to elevate social life to a higher grade; and to bring the whole power of mental culture to bear upon our countrymen." Membership was narrowly defined as graduates only. The duties of the officers were to compile an accurate list

Reunion head-quarters organized by class in 1911.

of graduates including their birth, graduation, and death dates, and to select an alumnus to deliver a public address or sermon at annual meetings held in conjunction with Commencement exercises.

The initial success faded quickly with the advent of the Civil War, and the Association had to be reorganized in 1868. In fact, the new secretary reported that the original Constitution and minutes of 1858 had disappeared, only to be "rescued from oblivion on the northern frontier of the great state of Texas." The revitalized association published a directory of ninety-two members in 1868 and quickly tackled pressing problems. In an attempt to improve student life, negotiations were entered into with students who were organizing illegal secret campus societies. The result was the installation of local chapters of three national fraternities: Chi Phi in 1871; Alpha Tau Omega in 1872; and Kappa Sigma in 1873. A Trinity Loan Association also was begun to assist needy students during the dire economic times of Reconstruction.

Vitally concerned about the future of Trinity College, the Alumni Association did not hesitate to confront the Board of Trustees over the issue of governance. Deploring too many political appointments to the Board, the Alumni Association began challenging the Trustees to appoint more "warm friends," a euphemism for alumni, to its membership. That victory dramatically was won when a new state charter, adopted in 1891, required that one-third, or twelve, of the members of the Board of Trustees be alumni of the college. Shortly thereafter, all students, whether graduates or not, were declared members of the Alumni Association. The increased roll included many prominent, successful men previously excluded from participating in the affairs of the Association. According to President Crowell, the change in the make-up of the Board of Trustees created "the most balanced Board in viewpoint" in the history of the institution.

Though desirable, and sometimes discussed as an official emphasis, fund raising was not a focus of the Association. With annual dues of fifty cents per member, the Association was as hard pressed to meet expenses as the college. Nevertheless the first fund raising appeal to alumni proved successful. After the controversial relocating of the college to Durham in 1892, the first major expansion of the original physical plant included the construction of a public auditorium. In an obvious plan to recognize the rich nineteenth-century heritage of the college, the new auditorium was designated as Craven Memorial Hall. An editorial in the *Christian Educator* in August, 1897, implored the supporters of Trinity College to rally and build the Memorial Hall before the following June. "If you love her, Brethren," the editorialist said, "Plank down the cash." The alumni raised $10,000 and the auditorium was ready for Commencement exercises in 1899. A repeat performance occurred in 1918 when friends and alumni raised $75,000 to construct Memorial Gymnasium, so named in honor of twenty-two students and alumni who died in World War I. After 1972 the building became more commonly known as the East Campus Gym.

As Trinity College prospered with the continued support of the Duke family, demands on the Alumni Association increased. An Alumnae Association was organized in 1912 to accommodate an increasing number of women graduates. To facilitate communication with an ever-expanding membership, a monthly publi-

The Alumni Association shared addresses and letters of alumni in service with the campus community during World War II.

cation, the *Trinity Alumni Register*, was begun in April, 1915. An Alumni Council was elected in 1917 to help in developing policy for the growing Association. The need for permanent, full-time oversight was recognized in 1920 with the employment of Bascom W. Barnard, '15, as the first Alumni Secretary. By 1924, a News Service was created and a Field Secretary was requested to maintain contact with approximately fifty local alumni associations. Fortunately, at the time when Trinity College became Duke University and all campus responsibilities significantly increased, the Alumni Association was prepared to meet the challenge. Almost since the inception of the college, alumni have been organized to assist the institution in defining and achieving its goals.

The University's Motto and Seal Haven't Avoided Controversy and Misspelling

The history of the seal and motto of Duke University has been mercurial with an unpredictable changeableness through the years. With the adoption of a shield, primarily for marketing, the official seal is not as visible as it used to be. However, the seal is carved in stone at several places on both East and West Campus. The seal is circular with Duke University in Latin and the motto, Eruditio et Religio, around the outer edge. The interior design consists of a wreath composed of two different kinds of leaves with a cross with rays of light behind it in the center.

There is no official record of the adoption of the seal even though the use of one is authorized by the charter of 1851. The earliest extant examples of the seal are on diplomas in 1869 and a bank loan in 1883. The first printed representation of the seal and motto is on an invitation to the commencement exercises of 1889. An early institutional history by Bruce Craven, grandson of President Braxton Craven, notes that President Craven selected the motto in 1859 at the time the name of the college was changed to Trinity. Braxton Craven stated that "for a church college, the name Trinity included everything that a church college ought to stand for, and that with the motto, formed a consistent plan of Christian education."

The motto most probably originated from a Methodist hymn by Charles Wesley, brother of the founder of Methodism, John Wesley. Titled "Sanctified Knowledge" in the contemporary pre-Civil War hymnal, the third stanza begins, "Unite the pair so long disjoined, Knowledge and vital piety...." Further proof that the hymn was well-known by the founders of the college is that another phrase from the hymn, "ignorance and error," appears in the preamble of the constitution of Union Institute, a name of the institution before it became Trinity College. The desire to join education and religion in a common endeavor is not at all surprising when one remembers that Methodism originated on the campus of Oxford University when John and Charles Wesley were students, and that one of the worldwide legacies of the Methodist Church is the founding of institutions of higher education. In North

The official university seal with the Latin revision of 1957.

Carolina the most prevalent form of higher education was sponsored by the church. The Methodists, Baptists, Presbyterians and Quakers each founded institutions known today as Duke University, Greensboro College, Wake Forest University, Davidson College, and Guilford College in the 1830s.

The first reference to the seal in the minutes of the board of trustees is a curious handwritten note dated May, 1888, by the new president, John Franklin Crowell. Crowell emphatically stated that the Latin on the present seal was indefensible and that he would not sign a diploma using it as "it would be a reflection on my scholarship." This comment was followed with the bold command, "Get a new seal." After the change of name to Duke University in 1924, the Latin inscription read Sigillum Universitatis Dukensis which was changed again in 1957 to Universitas Dukiana. Apparently the designers of the seal have had difficulty agreeing on the proper Latin through the years.

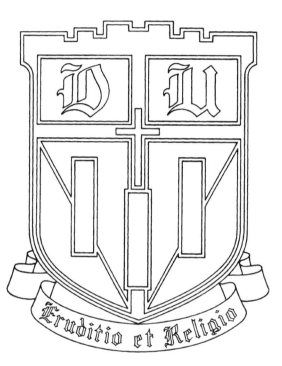

President Douglas M. Knight initiated a study of university symbols in 1964 which implemented far-reaching changes. A committee consisting of representatives from the medical center and the art department composed an official shield designed for use on a variety of commercial products where the seal was thought to be inappropriate. The shape of the shield is patterned after the Duke family crest with the notched top inspired by the roof lines of the Gothic architecture of West Campus. A triangle, the symbol of unity and the Trinity, is incorporated within the borders of the shield, with the theme further emphasized by the repetition of three vertical bars representing education, religion, and health. This is the first time the concept of health is visually introduced in a university symbol. The motto is repeated on a ribbon beneath the shield. With the approval of the new shield, the seal was reserved for use only by authorization of the board of trustees. Additional committees at the same time recommended the design of a Duke flag, the designation of an official shade of Duke blue, the authorization of an official distinctive Duke doctoral cap, gown and hood, and the design of an official chain of office and mace for use by the president.

The official university shield adopted in 1964.

The aims of the university date from bylaws prepared by President John C. Kilgo at the request of the board of trustees in 1903. When Trinity College became the undergraduate school of the new institution, Duke University, in 1924, the aims, motto and seal of the college were adopted and thus continued by the university. The aims of the university are most prominently displayed on a bronze plaque in the main quadrangle of West Campus which was a gift of alumni. The plaque was dedicated at Homecoming Weekend in 1942.

In 1993 the university telephone directory had on its cover a striking color photograph of the pediment above the entrance to Baldwin Auditorium on East Campus which depicted the seal of the university. Taken with a telephoto lens, the close-up image of the motto revealed the stonecutter's misspelling of the Latin word Religio! Thus a permanent reminder of the difficulty with the Latin in the official seal through the years is displayed for all to see. The prominent cover touched off a flurry of correspondence in the *Chronicle* over the "newly discovered" seal of the university. Some writers thought it to be politically incorrect while others defended it as quite appropriate. Also, many references over the decades have attributed the origin of certain university symbols to either Washington or James B. Duke. What we know of the origin of the seal, motto and aims of the university are attributable to the actions of the board of trustees in the context of the history of the institution from its inception in 1838. Discussion is always welcome about university symbols but it should be based on an accurate understanding of the institution's history.

The seal carved in stone over Baldwin Auditorium with the original Latin version and "Religio" misspelled in the motto.

The Civil War Experience

In 1865, the institution now called Duke University voluntarily closed its doors for the only time in its history. Ironically it temporarily ceased operation not because of fighting or the uncertainty of political reconstruction but because of the surrender of a Confederate army headquartered on its campus and encamped throughout the community. The Civil War brought excitement, uncertainty, and a desperate struggle for survival but Trinity College, unlike many southern institutions, managed to remain open throughout the war.

The academic year 1860–61 opened with great promise. The student enrollment of 215 represented the second largest total in history with the boarding capacity of the community stretched to its limit. As a consequence, the trustees approved President Braxton Craven's ambitious plans for an impressive new building which included dormitory space for the first time. However, with the firing on Fort Sumter in April, 1861, and the secession of North Carolina in response to President Lincoln's call for troops, the history of the school was altered forever. Opening enrollment dropped to eighty-two in 1862 as students rushed off to enlist in the militia with their friends. Only six seniors remained to graduate the following spring.

Anticipating such a decline, President Craven organized a student-based military unit, called the Trinity Guard, in an attempt to retain students. The Guard

This ambrotype of the college military unit, the Trinity Guard, taken around 1861, is the oldest photographic image in the University Archives.

invested in uniforms, drilled over the summer and even marched to a few communities to show the flag in an attempt to quiet local pro-Union sentiment. In November, Craven took the Trinity Guard to nearby Salisbury where he had accepted command of the recently formed Confederate prison. His commission was offered by the Governor of North Carolina and he considered the unit part of the home guard, but the Confederate Secretary of War ruled otherwise placing the men in the regular army subject to assignment anywhere in the Confederacy. With the reason for the Trinity Guard thus negated, Craven resigned his command and returned to the college with the few boys too young to be subject to the already expanding draft laws.

In 1863 the college opened with forty students, its smallest enrollment ever. Only one senior graduated that year. By 1864 most of the students were in the preparatory department and fifteen to twenty women were admitted to boost enrollment. W. T. Gannaway, Professor of Latin and Greek, characterized the presence of women in his class as "an oasis in the Sahara of War."

John Franklin Heitman (1840–1904), enrolled as a student in 1861 but left immediately to join the Confederate army. He graduated after the war and became Professor of Greek, German, Metaphysics and Theology at Trinity in 1883.

Wartime changed college life drastically. At first, change was more patriotic as the Columbian Literary Society purchased portraits of Jefferson Davis and P. G. T. Beauregard to replace those of Winfield Scott and Lewis Cass which they "consigned to the flames." But as the war dragged on financial concerns overrode all else. Board increased from $25 to $40 and then $80 and finally $200 per month. Payment in kind became the norm. For example, John B. Yarborough, a wounded soldier, paid for three months board with seven bushels of wheat and 250 pounds of salt. Even though alumni donated old books, students still had to be asked to bring whatever textbooks they could find with them.

Among the faculty one professor performed as much work as two or three, subsisting by farming in addition to teaching. Salaries were "whatever might be made," meaning the limited college income was divided among the faculty. Braxton Craven noted in his diary, "A hard life it is in every sense. No wonder so very few colleges live."

As conditions worsened events rushed to a climax in the spring of 1865. The hated Confederate collection of produce so stripped the county that college authorities appealed to President Jefferson Davis for a limited exemption in order to be able to support even a small enrollment. Before a reply arrived the Confederate capital of Richmond fell to General Grant, and Davis and his cabinet fled southward. From the opposite direction the Confederate army of General Joseph E. Johnston was in full retreat before General William T. Sherman who was advancing northwestward. An advance division of Johnston's retreating army under General W. M. Hardee arrived at Trinity using the campus for headquarters. Professor Gannaway described the army which stretched out for six miles along the main road as "20,000 half-clad and half-fed soldiers with thousands of perishing horses. " The men were well be-haved, he noted, but it was obvious to him that "we were at the mercy of our foes." When word arrived that peace was negotiated at the not-too-distant Durham's Station, the college bell summoned the community for the announce-ment. Gannaway described the scene, "The gladdened shouts at the thought of peace, home and friends made the welkin ring. It was springtime, in the month of May."

Despite the promise of peace and springtime, the rural community proved too decimated for quick recovery. The college campus was in a sad state of neglect and badly in need of repair. Authorities first announced an indefinite suspension and then struck a positive note declaring that "exercises would be resumed on the first Wednesday of January, 1866." The college duly opened as announced and the school prospered sufficiently to begin an addition to the main building by April, 1871. It was a triumph just to continue to operate and exist during the Civil War and Reconstruction. However, the ambitious plans envisioned before the war never materialized. If they had, perhaps Trinity College would have been too firmly rooted in Randolph County to ever contemplate removal at a later date.

Marquis Lafayette Wood:
The Overlooked President _____

In the 1970s when the secretary to the university mounted photographs of the presidents of Trinity College and Duke University in the board room in Allen Building, a forgotten president received long overdue recognition. Marquis Lafayette Wood who served as duly elected president of Trinity College from June, 1883, until January, 1885, had been largely overlooked because of the brevity of his tenure during tumultuous times. Wood's term was sandwiched between a period when the chairman of the faculty, W. H. Pegram, administered college affairs following the sudden death of Braxton Craven and the critical assumption of administration by a committee of management consisting of three wealthy Methodist laymen. Preceded and followed by such dominating personalities as Craven and Julian S. Carr, James A. Gray, and John W. Alspaugh, Wood became lost in transition. Yet Marquis (pronounced Marcus) Lafayette Wood's overall career is fascinating and his presidential term was not without significance. Interestingly, among a dozen leaders Wood is the only alumnus to serve as president in Duke's history.

Born in the local community in 1829, the tenth of fourteen children, Wood worked on his father's farm until age twenty-one when he enrolled in Union Institute which became a college during his attendance. Wood epitomized the kind of student Craven believed the college existed to serve. Converted at a nearby Methodist camp meeting and licensed to preach, Wood fervently believed that education and religion were vital components in bettering one's lot. Carefully kept diaries reveal that after ordination Wood meticulously followed the requirements of the Methodist Church. He sought out and preached to slaves, distributed church literature, and founded Sabbath Schools which often taught reading and writing as well when ten or more children were present in a congregation.

Wood never missed commencement exercises at his alma mater and in 1859 at a missionary meeting during commencement week, he answered a call to be the first missionary to China from the North Carolina Conference. He married Ellen Morphis, a faculty member at nearby Greensboro College, and they sailed from New York City on a seven-month voyage to Shanghai, China. His missionary service came at a most unpropitious time. Besieged by the Tai-ping Rebellion in China and cut off from communication from home by the Civil War, he had to find secular employment for financial support. He assiduously studied Chinese, preaching in the native language and earning income as a translator for cotton brokers. With two small children to support alone after his wife's untimely death, Wood returned home at the first opportunity in 1866. Rejoining his local conference, Wood received church appointments throughout the state. He immediately renewed his college ties and was elected to the Board of Trustees in 1873.

When Wood became president in 1883, the college had a debt of $6,786 and assets, "as supposed to be good" of only $1,903.60. Enrollment dropped from 100 to 60 in a year, with ten of those students receiving free tuition and eight given permission to pay "on time." Wood worked extremely hard at rebuilding confidence in the school through preaching and lecturing throughout the state. Believing there to be an abundance of money in the tobacco section of North Carolina, he even led a modest beginning at raising the first endowment ever for the college. Wood, however, had difficulty with the faculty. Professor John F. Heitman alluded to the problem when he stated, "The government of the college is in the faculty, the president being the executive officer." Wood became inundated with administrative detail, including the disciplining of students, and he became embroiled in a controversy over whether to pay off debt or raise endowment.

Marquis Lafayette Wood (1829–1893) raised the first money for endowment and held the school together as president for a year-and-a-half after Craven's death in 1882. He is the only alumnus to serve as president of the institution.

Wood's legacy is that he understood the long-term interest of the college and held it together over the short term. In his final report to the trustees he wrote, "The history of Trinity College is peculiar. It is the product principally of one man, Braxton Craven. His genius and indomitable energy built it up and he gave it to the church." Both Craven and Wood understood that if the school were to survive it would be through identification with and support from the Methodist Church. Close to home they saw developing parallel histories for Davidson College with the Presbyterian Church and Wake Forest College with the Baptist Church. Wood also knew that when nineteenth-century institutions became closely identified with the personality of a particular long-time leader, they more often than not succumbed as well at the death of that president. Wood fervently believed in the Methodist Church with its emphasis on the uniting of knowledge and piety as its founder John Wesley expressed it. Craven had institutionalized the concept with the school's motto, Eruditio et Religio. Wood also astutely reminded the trustees that, "All great enterprises require time and patience and labor and suffering and money." Wood devoted a lifetime of time, patience, labor, and suffering to his alma mater, even stepping aside as president when the offer of money seemed eminent if the management of the college were entrusted to wealthy laymen of the church. He remained a member of the board of trustees throughout his life, ironically submitting the resolution in 1889 that authorized the removal of the college from his beloved native county to the city of Durham. That move also brought spectacular financial support from yet another layman honoring commitment to the teaching of his church. Perhaps Wood heard the suggestion, uttered in frustration and maybe jest, of a financial agent of the college who said, "Trinity should go to the Dukes and become Duke College." That development, however, remained for another generation and another time. But today it is entirely proper and overdue that Marquis Lafayette Wood be recognized as a worthy leader in the list of presidents of Duke University.

_____ Julian S. Carr: Duke's Forgotten Benefactor

Julian Shakespeare Carr, Durham industrialist and philanthropist, has, perhaps, a unique distinction in the history of higher education in North Carolina. He is probably the only person to have served on the board of trustees of Trinity College and the University of North Carolina and to have a building named after him on both the Duke and Carolina campuses. As an alumnus of the state university, Carr never lost his affection for his alma mater. However, as a Methodist and passionate believer in the value of education, he also developed pride and labored long and hard for Trinity College, his church's institution of higher education.

Although Carr played a crucial role in the relocation of Trinity College to his beloved city of Durham, it is ironic that his greatest contributions to Trinity occurred when it was in rural Randolph County. Once the college became the primary focus of the philanthropy of the Duke family, Carr's contributions slipped into obscurity. In truth, there would be no Duke University if Carr had not lent his name, prestige, administrative talent, and money to Trinity College as it struggled to survive in the post-Civil War south.

Born in 1845, Carr was the son of a Chapel Hill merchant. His student days at the state university were interrupted by service as a private in the Confederate Army. Late in life he was always known as General Carr, a rank won through long, devoted service in Confederate veterans' affairs. After the war, Carr's father helped him become a partner in the tobacco manufacturing firm of W. T. Blackwell and Company in nearby Durham. His business acumen led to the firm becoming known worldwide through its instantly recognizable Bull Durham trademark. The town's citizens certainly knew the origin of their fame as the factory's "whistle" sounded the bellow of a bull daily. Carr became one of the state's wealthiest individuals, reportedly its first millionaire, later engaging in successful textile, banking, railroad, public utility, and newspaper endeavors.

As Trinity College struggled to overcome post-war dependency on uncertain student tuition and church donations, interested Meth-

Julian S. Carr (1845–1924), reportedly the state's first millionaire, was Durham's first successful tobacco entrepreneur and Trinity's major benefactor before Washington Duke.

odist laymen were crucial to its survival. Carr's name first appears in college records signing a note to forestall foreclosure on a mortgage due in 1880. He was elected a trustee in 1883 at the critical time following the death of longtime president, Braxton Craven. Heavily in debt and perhaps too dependent upon the prestige of the late president, Trinity faced a very uncertain future. At a time when unity appeared vital, Methodist support split in a public debate over whether to pay off debt or create an endowment as the best means to assure the future of the college. Carr agreed to be one of twenty persons to contribute $5,000 each to establish a permanent endowment fund. However, the effort failed miserably.

Carr next proposed a radical remedy to save the college. At the annual conference of the Methodist church in 1884, he proposed that the administration of the college be transferred to a Committee of Management consisting of J. W. Alspaugh, chairman of the trustees; himself, as treasurer of the board; and James A. Gray, an alumnus from Winston. The three would leave the title of the property with the church, administer in the name of the current board of trustees, begin an endowment campaign, and guarantee $5,000 over the next two years for the operation of the school. Although the endowment campaign failed once again, the plan of day-to-day management succeeded and the college survived. At Christmas in 1886, Carr personally donated a $1,000 bonus for faculty salaries.

Aside from the plan of management, Carr made three outstanding contributions toward the success of the school. In June, 1887, he gave $10,000 for endowment which at that time was the largest donation in the history of the institution. As chairman of the committee to nominate a president, he engineered the selection of John F. Crowell who surprisingly was neither a preacher, nor a Methodist, nor even a southerner. One of Crowell's many accomplishments was to win support for the removal of Trinity College from its rural setting to the manufacturing city of Durham. Carr helped make the move a reality by donating sixty-two acres of land for the new site. His donation along with Washington Duke's gift of $85,000 for buildings and endowment changed the history of the school forever. Julian S. Carr clearly deserves recognition as one of the schools primary benefactors.

Carr dormitory opened in 1927 as part of the new Georgian-style Woman's College campus.

President John F. Crowell Left Lasting Mark on the University

At the end of the nineteenth century Trinity College was led by one of its most significant presidents, John Franklin Crowell. He was our first modern, or "twentieth century," president even though he served from 1887 to 1894. If cited at all today, he usually is mentioned only for being the one responsible for moving the college to Durham. However, Crowell was far from a one-dimensional president.

President John F. Crowell (1857–1931).

In the mid-1880s the college floundered after the death of Braxton Craven who had presided over the school for forty-two years. Saved from extinction by a Committee of Management of three wealthy Methodist businessmen (Julian S. Carr of Durham and James A. Gray and John W. Alspaugh of Winston), the college truly was at a crossroads. The poverty of war and reconstruction had dealt a severe blow to higher education in the South and as the traditional private colleges and state universities struggled to, in effect, begin anew, they faced competition from a new kind of institution with a decidedly practical emphasis. In North Carolina, for Trinity and the University of North Carolina, the new competition came from the Agricultural and Mechanical College in Raleigh (now NCSU), the Normal and Industrial College for Women (now UNC-Greensboro) and several teacher-training institutions scattered across the state. In selecting a new president for Trinity, the Methodists, one perceptive observer noted, had to choose between the traditional path of "a favorite clergyman of proved piety and conservatism, or a young man trained in the study of economic and social needs of the day." Perhaps to the surprise of many, the selection committee took the chance of a new direction.

The trustees offered the presidency to Crowell, a young man aged 29 with scant experience, who was a northerner by birth and training and, although a minister, not even a Methodist. The unlikely candidate was, as a graduate student,

the boxing partner at Yale of Horace Williams of Chapel Hill who recommended him to his father-in-law, Julian S. Carr, who was chairman of the trustee search committee. Born in York, Pennsylvania, Crowell attended Dartmouth College before transferring to Yale where he earned a B.A. degree in 1883. After serving as principal of Schuylkill Seminary in Pennsylvania, Crowell returned to Yale for study in both the Divinity and Graduate Schools. While ordained in the Evangelical Church, his interests were in the study of the relatively new disciplines of economics and sociology. Crowell's first publication, a copy of which he mailed to Carr, was a study of the rapidly growing industrial employment of children published in the *Andover Review* in 1885. The farsighted trustees saw in Crowell the type of progressive educator that was needed to lead the college in a new era.

Crowell first saw Trinity when he began his presidency at Commencement exercises in 1887. In truth, he confided in his diary, he almost resigned and returned north. However, the impression he made was positive. One gentleman liked him because "he didn't try to tell them everything he knew." One thing he wisely did not tell immediately was that he noticed incorrect Latin on the college seal presented to him as his badge of office.

President Crowell and Professor Joseph L. Armstrong, who was hired at the same time, immediately set out to establish a new curriculum at Trinity. Armstrong had studied at Johns Hopkins University and the University of Leipzig. Together they had attended prestigious universities then undergoing curriculum reform themselves.

Basically they sought to replace the 19th-century model based on memorization with the developing German university model of learning based on research and independent thought. Recitations continued where mastery of details were necessary but oral and written examinations on general principles greatly increased. Investigations in primary sources such as public laws and documents, journals and newspapers were required and the practices of note taking, classroom discussion, and collateral reading became commonplace. To support the new emphasis on research, Crowell persuaded the competitive debating societies to merge their separate closed libraries into the college's first general library. Crowell personally catalogued the books and served selected hours as reference librarian to encourage and instruct the students in proper research methods.

The lively academic activity resulted in increased visiting lecturers and public discussion of current topics including the publication of a series of pamphlets as Trinity College Publications which often addressed issues before the state legislature. The students began their own literary magazine, *The Archive*, credited today as the second oldest such publication in the country. Other student initiatives included the founding of a Trinity College Historical Society which gave impetus to the beginning of a manuscript collection in the library and a select honorary society called 9019, a precursor of Phi Beta Kappa.

All of Crowell's emphasis was not academic. He strongly believed in physical fitness and he encouraged intramural competition in baseball, tennis, and lacrosse. When students sought his assistance in beginning intercollegiate competition in football he readily agreed, actually coaching the team for several years. Crowell had detected an economic and geographic division on campus between

When President Crowell introduced and coached football in 1887, the first Trinity team adopted the dark blue and white colors of Yale University, his alma mater, in gratitude.

eastern and up-country or supposedly richer and poorer students. He seized upon football as the best way to unite the student body as well as a way to challenge the prestige of the state university in Chapel Hill. When Trinity triumphed over UNC 16–0 in their first football encounter on Thanksgiving Day in 1887, Crowell, the college community, and its alumni basked in the attention given them by the state's press.

While principal of Schuylkill Seminary, Crowell had witnessed its removal from an urban setting in Reading to a rural one in Fredericksburg, a move he considered detrimental to the school. At Trinity, he believed the changes set in motion could be sustained only in a progressive city in the then popular image of the New South. Again, much to the surprise of many, the trustees agreed with Crowell and put the relocation of the college up for bids. Raleigh was selected initially as the favored site but Durham topped Raleigh's bid with the financial backing of Washington Duke and donation of land by Julian S. Carr. When plans were made to open a new campus in Durham in September, 1891, Crowell's transformation of the school seemed complete.

However, fate was to deal unkindly with Crowell. The tower of the new main building collapsed shortly before school was to open postponing the removal until 1892. Then the most severe economic depression in the history of the country further dealt a blow to his expansionist dreams. Disgruntled faculty resigned as promises of salary increases failed to materialize and opposition within the church surfaced, some of it attributed to latent antipathy to his northern background.

Crowell resigned as president in 1894. He served as head of the Department of Economics and Sociology at Smith College before studying at the University of Berlin and earning his Ph.D. degree from Columbia University in 1897. Then he began a second distinguished career as an economist, associate editor of the Wall Street Journal, and statistician in several positions in Washington, D.C. and New York. In 1917 Trinity College awarded him an honorary LL.D. degree. He lived until 1931, proudly observing the dramatic transformation of Trinity College into Duke University, a process he launched in no small measure himself.

A Place Called Home: Duke Homestead Reflects History of the Family That Created a University

Having the Duke family homestead, the birthplace of the institution's primary benefactors, in the same town as the university places Duke University in a unique position. In the history of American higher education, this cannot be said of such notable benefactors as John Harvard, Elihu Yale, Cornelius Vanderbilt, William Marsh Rice, or Leland Stanford. Visiting the Duke Homestead, a state historic site operated as a living history farm and tobacco museum, gives one a sense of the lifestyle of the Duke family. Coupled with a visit to the nearby university which bears the family name, one develops a special appreciation for a family's commitment to its church and community and the role of personal philanthropy in the development of higher education and the state. A careful look at what the home place and university represents is instructive.

In a very real sense Washington Duke's life was both typical and atypical of his generation. Before the Civil War, he lived the typical life of the southern yeoman farmer. Born in 1820, the eighth of ten children with little opportunity for schooling, his life centered around family, church and making a living from often less than ideal farming conditions. His chief assets were solid values anchored in family and church, a strong physical body, and a willingness to work hard. His life was not without success or tragedy. Starting out renting land, he accumulated 300 acres by gift through marriage or purchase. In 1852 he built a modest four-room frame house with a detached kitchen. Widowed with two children, he remarried, adding three more children to the family, only to lose his second wife and one child to typhoid fever. Like many in his class, he opposed the coming of the Civil War, yet he dutifully served at age forty-three when the Confederacy raised the draft age to forty-five. Returning home after the war, he happily collected his children from scattered family members and began life anew. In an interview at the end of a successful life, he said he felt desperately poor twice, once when he began farming on his own and again at the end of the war when he had to start all over.

For Washington Duke, 1865 was a pivotal year. Declaring he had plowed more furrows in God's earth than any man his age, he turned to the manufacture of tobacco for a living. In reality manufacturing simply meant hard hand labor of a different sort, and it clearly was a family enterprise. Duke and his children flailed, sifted, and packed cured Bright Leaf tobacco into small cloth bags with hand lettered tags reading "Pro Bono Publico," — for the public good. Traveling by wagon and camping by the roadside, Duke and his son, James Buchanan or "Buck," began peddling the family manufactured smoking and chewing tobacco throughout eastern North Carolina. Success soon required the need for a second and even third factory at the homestead. In 1874 a desire to be near the railroad necessitated a move into the growing town of Durham.

Today at the forty-five acre farmstead one may visit the original farmhouse, a curing barn, a pack house, and the first and third factories alongside a cultivated field of tobacco and vegetables. Open to the public with a regular posted schedule, the homestead comes alive at special times throughout the year when costumed guides illustrate working the land, curing and auctioning tobacco, performing family chores, hosting a circuit riding preacher, and decorating for Christmas. It is easy to visualize and even participate in activities typical of a small southern farm in the 1870s. In the adjoining museum one can follow the history of the planting, harvesting, curing, manufacturing and marketing of tobacco. Especially interesting are interactive exhibits of a talking mannequin tobacco farmer working in the field, the recorded chant of a tobacco auctioneer, and a series of televised cigarette advertisements. Lest one question the authenticity of the museum, anti-tobacco sentiments from England's King James I to the United States' Surgeon General are presented as well.

The Duke Homestead, built in 1852, is the birthplace of Washington Duke's second family. The Homestead, donated by the university to the state, is an historic site open to the public.

The Duke family became atypical in the post-Civil War era. The region's unique Bright Leaf tobacco and the family's products became so popular that Washington ultimately was peddling products in thirty-two states. His son, James Buchanan, left Durham to open a factory in New York where his genius for business organization led him to build a worldwide tobacco empire through the American and the British-American Tobacco Companies. When the United States government broke up the tobacco trust through enforcement of the Sherman Antitrust Act in 1911, J. B. Duke hardly felt the effect for by then he had launched a second business career building dams for the production of electricity in Canada and in North and South Carolina.

Converted at a revival at a young age, Washington Duke was a devout Methodist. He enjoyed good preaching, supported the benevolences of the church, and gladly helped the less fortunate. Late in life his church's school, Trinity College, became the primary focus of his philanthropy when he gave $85,000 to relocate the school to Durham. His children followed his example with Benjamin beginning annual contributions to the college in 1889 and James B. making his first large donation in 1902. In 1924, James B. Duke formalized the family's lifetime of giving by creating the Duke Endowment, a philanthropic institution designed to aid higher education, hospitals, orphanages, and the Methodist Church in North and South Carolina. At the same time he donated $17 million for the construction of a new campus for a new university to be built around Trinity College and named after his father and family.

At a sophomore class picnic at the Duke Homestead, a student was heard to exclaim, "So this is the Duke plantation." Though wealthy by post-war standards Washington Duke certainly was not a member of the pre-war planter class. His life dramatically illustrates that one can triumph over tragedy, and that hard work has its rewards. Washington Duke was one of the South's first native-born philanthropists and his sons, particularly, James B., carried on the tradition in a spectacular fashion. Just three miles from the homestead stands the university that publicizes the family name around the world. Duke University has grown from a college of 134 students and faculty of 17 that relocated to Durham in 1892 to a major research institution of approximately 11,000 students and faculty of 1,600. Rarely is one able to observe the spectacular legacy of a single family so vividly in the same locale as that of the Dukes in Durham.

Durham's Winning Bid for Trinity College

Over one hundred years ago in March, 1890, the Board of Trustees met to accept Washington Duke's offer to relocate Trinity College to Durham. That turn of events was surprising for three reasons. First, when President John F. Crowell initially broached the idea of relocating the college, the almost universal response was "the Methodist preachers would never allow it." Second, when cities competed for the college, Raleigh was selected as the new site. Third, while devout Methodists, the Duke family had demonstrated little interest in higher education as a focus of its philanthropy.

In 1887 when the twenty-nine-year-old Crowell became president of Trinity the then fifty-year-old institution acquired a man of vision and self-confidence. The college itself consisted of a single impressive all-purpose building located seventy miles west of Durham in Randolph County. An affiliation with the Methodist Church provided most of its students. While proud of their institution, the Methodists were more adept at launching campaigns to raise money than providing steady hard cash.

Crowell appealed to the pride and loyalty of the church and alumni to accomplish the relocation of the college. His guiding philosophy was to put "modern learning at the service of the people under the auspices of Christian truth."

Trinity College in Randolph County, pictured around 1890, consisted of a single all-purpose building. Students boarded in the homes of faculty and local farmers.

This active interjection of learning, religion and service into the popular consciousness could best be accomplished, he believed, in an urban setting. After all, there was neither a railroad, telegraph nor telephone within five miles of the college. He firmly believed that if the college were to survive the rapidly changing conditions of the New South and acquire prestige and power, growth was imperative. Such growth had failed to materialize in its rural setting. Over the course of a year Crowell's views gradually triumphed in a skillfully conducted debate in the official church bodies that were empowered to decide the issue.

With the church on record as willing to move the college, the question shifted to which urban locales might be interested. The Trustees determined that it would take $20,500 to replace the present building plus obtain a suitable site. Having recently been selected for the Baptist Female Seminary (now Meredith College), Raleigh was prepared to compete again. A site now occupied by North Carolina State University was offered and citizens of Raleigh pledged $35,000 for a building. The Methodist Conference overwhelmingly voted approval.

Quietly, and unknown to President Crowell, Methodist ministers in Durham had been approaching Washington Duke on behalf of a significant benefaction to the church, presumably to Trinity College. Mary Duke Lyon, Duke's only daughter, wished for her father to remember the church as well. "For certain," Trustee H. T. Bass reported later, "the Dukes never made any considerable contribution without satisfying themselves that the cause was fully worthy of their aid." Indeed, unknown to college authorities Washington Duke had attended Trinity commencement the previous spring. In December, 1889, Benjamin N. Duke, Washington's son, was elected to the Trinity Board of Trustees. Ben's election represented the honored tradition of recognizing dedicated, wealthy laymen and the historical record does not reveal whether it had any relation to the impending relocation of the school. Nevertheless it was a timely appointment.

An advertisement for the new college in Durham.

TRINITY COLLEGE INN, Durham, N. C.

A Model College Home: Furnished Dormitories, Dining Room, Parlors, Chapel, Bath-Rooms, Water Closets, Sewerage System, City Water Supply, Electric Lights from College Electric Plant, Warm Air Heating. Located in a grove on the College Grounds. The gift of Mr. Washington Duke, of Durham.

After conference approval of the Raleigh site things moved swiftly in Durham. When Washington Duke's former pastor and then District Superintendent E. A. Yates told him of Raleigh's offer Duke casually remarked that Durham could match that and add $50,000 for endowment. Yates inquired if he could wire Crowell such an offer and immediately the college president was in Durham personally meeting Washington Duke for the first time. With a pledge from Duke of $85,000 in hand, Yates and Crowell hurried across town to ask their friend Julian S. Carr, long-time trustee and the largest benefactor of the college to date, if he would donate as a site the fairground he owned on the western edge of the city. Carr agreed without hesitation.

When called to meet in Durham on March 20, the trustees accepted the offers from Duke and Carr with gratitude. The formal offer from Duke was signed by Washington but written by Benjamin. As further inducement citizens from Durham presented a check for $9,361 for endowment and the trustees enthusiastically proclaimed that with Duke's gift for endowment and a building, funds were ample for a solid beginning. Upon request, a committee from Raleigh relinquished its claim and the *Christian Advocate,* the official organ of the church, proclaimed, "All Methodists could write the address Trinity College, Durham, North Carolina with pride."

The new beginning given Trinity College by Washington Duke in 1890 blossomed into another dramatic departure in 1924. That thrust into university status was based on the solid foundation of an outstanding liberal arts college and on the continued positive focus of the service of education to the church and especially to the region and nation as envisioned by President William P. Few and James B. Duke.

Durham Opening Postponed: When the Tower Came Tumbling Down

In September, 1892, Trinity College opened in Durham. It had been slated to open a year earlier in 1891. Why did it not open as planned? Because the dramatic collapse of the tower of the main college building just weeks before classes were to begin postponed the move. With the center third of the most important building in ruins, the administration had no choice but to continue school another year in Randolph County. The calamity also threatened to undo the carefully constructed plans implementing the relocation.

Suddenly student enrollment and the vital income from tuition became uncertain. Cost overruns for construction, already a problem, became more acute with an undetermined amount of money needed for repair or rebuilding. And equally alarming, the settled debate over the wisdom of moving from the original rural setting to a new urban one threatened to reappear. When news of the tower's collapse circulated in the old Trinity community, some residents threw hats in the air in celebration, and others claimed it was an act of God to prevent removal.

The Washington Duke building, the main college administrative building in Durham prior to 1910.

Newspapers in High Point and Durham conducted a heated debate all over again about the merits of the respective sites for Trinity College.

As construction neared completion on the main building, rumors circulated that it was unsafe. Fearing damage to his reputation, the contractor asked President John F. Crowell to inspect the building with him. After a statement attesting to the building's safety appeared in the newspaper, fears subsided. But then a few weeks later on a Saturday afternoon the builder noticed a small crack in the tower archway which was the main entrance to the structure, and he instructed the foreman to dismiss the workers if the crack should widen. At around two o'clock Sunday morning the one-hundred-foot tower of the three-story brick building tumbled down, fortunately injuring no one.

The main building, later to be named the Washington Duke Building, was crucial to the operation of the college. The first floor contained classrooms, a chapel, and the office of the president. The second and third floors consisted of sixty dormitory rooms, each divided by a partition into a study and bedroom suite for two students. That innovative arrangement, plus indoor plumbing and a much publicized heating system, led to the boast of its being the "most complete college building in the state in point of architecture, ventilation, comfort and modern conveniences."

Benjamin N. Duke paid for an out-of-state architect to inspect the ruins, but in the interest of harmony a formal report ascribing blame never was issued. It was clear that faulty design as well as poorly prepared mortar caused the collapse. The architect and contractor were at fault and both of them had been selected and their work approved by the building committee of the trustees and the administration.

The heroes in bringing order out of the chaos, in President Crowell's opinion, were a group of local Durham businessmen—E.J. Parrish, Virginius Ballard, William H. Branson and B. N. Duke—who gave unselfishly of their time at the time of crisis. They met frequently and dealt wisely with issues of construction, finance and public relations. They ignored the silly debate which demeaned the other city rather than extolling one's own merits which raged in the High Point and Durham newspapers, never questioning the decision to move the college. Noting the loss in tuition revenue, they reduced faculty salaries, one of the largest expenditures, although the faculty claimed they were being charged disproportionately for financial concerns not of their making. They immediately began rebuilding the fallen tower, paying special attention to footings, the best hard brick available, the preparation of cement, and careful supervision.

The first college library on the new campus was in the Washington Duke building.

Trinity College experienced a quite unexpected and very difficult last year in Randolph County during 1891–1892. Unfortunately, as an economic depression spread throughout the land, the first year in Durham had its own unique set of problems, too. However, the suitability of the rebuilt Washington Duke building was not one of them. In fact when the building unexpectedly burned in 1910, all of the building collapsed except for the heavily reinforced tower.

The Move From a Rural Setting to the "New South" City of Durham

In 1892, everyone, not just entering students, began the college year with apprehension. September 1 marked the opening of Trinity College in Durham, thus ending a laborious three-year effort to relocate the college from its original site in Randolph County. That September the faculty and administration alike had mixed emotions about the move. Although desirable, it was not easy to leave the tranquil and comfortable rural surroundings of over fifty years for an urban setting and an unknown future. President John F. Crowell later wrote that even though it was less than one hundred miles from Randolph County to Durham, it was ten thousand miles away psychologically.

Everything was new. The items moved were meager indeed. A railroad box car transported the college bell, clock, safe and several thousand books while Professor Pegram's cow and President Crowell's carriage and saddle horses hoofed it. What had been a faculty of eight in 1890 became a faculty of seventeen in 1892. Only two professors, however, actually had taught classes in Randolph County. Most of the Old Trinity faculty preferred to remain on their farms taking a chance on the success of the high school to be opened in the vacated college building. As hoped for, Trinity College enrollment jumped from 113 to 180 with the change to Durham. President Crowell soon discovered that administratively the change was exacting. He reported there were "no traditions to go by. Every internal and external relationship had been changed. Every structural feature, every functional activity had to be readjusted to different requirements."

The contrast between the old campus and the new one was dramatic. In Old Trinity students lived in community boarding houses and the college consisted of a single all-purpose building. In Durham a more typical campus atmosphere prevailed. The spacious county fairground where trotting horses raced and steeple

A double-arched gate prominently displaying the school's motto marked the entrance to the college prior to 1915.

chases were held was converted to a park-like campus of three main buildings, seven residences for faculty, and athletic fields complete with a grandstand left over from the race track.

The Main Building, later named the Washington Duke Building, was a three-story brick building with a central bell and clock tower which faced Main Street. It contained offices, meeting rooms, classrooms, the college library and sixty dormitory rooms for students. An "imposing structure somewhat dull and heavy in appearance" to one observer, it burned in 1911 becoming the only campus building ever lost to fire.

Epworth Inn, a rambling wooden structure, was the most attractive building and the focus of student activity, probably because it contained dining and meeting facilities as well as seventy-five dormitory rooms. Its ample porches provided a home-like atmosphere for residents and visitors alike. Epworth still is used today but it is only about one-third of its original size.

The third public building which housed the School of Technology later was named the Crowell Science Building. A personal gift of President Crowell in honor of his wife who died at the time of the relocation of the college, the three-story brick building with a full basement contained a drafting room, and laboratories for chemistry, physics and biology. It also housed the generator which supplied electricity for the entire campus.

Married faculty were pleased with their houses, especially since they had indoor plumbing. Washington Duke, however, felt they were too small so he immediately had wrap-around porches added. Four of the original houses exist today in the adjoining Trinity Park residential area.

In strictly monetary terms the value of the college plant easily increased over ten times by relocation. However, to Crowell and the faculty and students attracted to Durham, the greatest gain by far was an intangible "newer outlook— the vastly extended vista of a new era." Despite the ever present adjustments the college community was excited over being "a part of change and progress and having a part to play in advancing into a higher and better order of life."

Progress was indeed evident. Five women enrolled the first year in Durham beginning an unbroken commitment by Trinity College to the education of women. It had been twelve years since the first and only women had graduated in 1878. The published roster listed two graduate and five law students as well. The overwhelming number of students were from North Carolina but South Carolina, the District of Columbia, and Indian Territory (now Oklahoma) were represented too. A national economic depression slowed matriculation from out-of-state but before long students began appearing from Virginia, Tennessee, Pennsylvania, and even Japan. Within a decade Trinity College clearly was attracting more and better students, decidedly greater financial support, and an impressive faculty. Crowell's ambitious vision for Trinity College was vindicated and a major foundation for Duke University was put in place.

_Washington Duke and the Education of Women

The early history of the education of women at Trinity always sparks debate. How committed was the administration to equality of education for men and women? Were women students second-class citizens relegated to private tutoring or non-resident status despite receiving the same diplomas as men? Unfortunately sufficient documentation to completely answer such questions simply does not exist. What *is* known has been the object of continual interpretation. Numerous articles and several outstanding honors' papers and dissertations on women at Duke make fascinating reading.

Washington Duke (1820–1905), family patriarch, is memorialized by a seated statue on East Campus.

Pivotal in this institutional debate is a letter from benefactor Washington Duke to President John C. Kilgo dated December 5, 1896. In this often-quoted letter, Duke pledges $100,000 to Trinity College for endowment provided the college "will open its doors to women placing them on an equal footing with men." The size of the gift, the fact of a proviso, and the subject of the letter gave rise to widespread publicity. Letters arrived praising the seventy-six-year-old gentleman for his support for women's rights. He even politely declined the offered position of vice president of the National Suffrage Association.

No documentation exists that explains the motivation for the restriction attached to the gift. The four women students already enrolled and about to graduate at the time of the announcement remarked much later that "Mr. Duke was always interested in us and would question us about our progress and chuckle over our achievements." A plausible explanation may be the desire to memorialize, although indirectly, the life of Mary Duke, Washington Duke's only daughter, who died at the age of forty. Only family members knew the extent of her caring for her widowed father and motherless brothers as well as her considerable help in launching the early tobacco enterprises.

From the institutional perspective, Trinity had already awarded diplomas to women. In 1878 three sisters, Mary, Persis, and Theresa Giles, earned A.B. degrees at old Trinity in Randolph County. Part of their instruction had been private tutoring and part had been in the classroom with men. Just why this was so has been the cause of much comment. However, with unique domestic and financial demands incident to their collegiate schooling at ages 25, 30, and 32, it is difficult to assess the reasons for a particular method of instruction. When approached, President Craven gladly accepted the Giles sisters as students. However, there was no pressure on Trinity to admit women since the Methodists operated a college for women in nearby Greensboro.

When the college opened in Durham in 1892 women were again admitted but as day students only. Three of the four enrolled were faculty children and it was their progress that Washington Duke followed closely. The practical effect of his restricted gift in 1896 was the immediate construction of a residential dormitory. It was proudly named the Mary Duke Building in honor of Duke's daughter.

Having a dorm dramatically increased the attractiveness of Trinity for women. However, the first year was controversial but not for the expected reasons. The dorm was finished so quickly it provided more beds than there were female students. President John C. Kilgo quietly picked suitable senior men to share the facility. A professor's wife wrote her daughter, "Dr. Kilgo has put boys in the Woman's Building so you see it has come down to a mixed boarding house already. If my girl was there I would take her away." Later records indicate this ironically co-ed dorm may have had nine male boarders, mostly single faculty. The Mary Duke dormitory, sparked by Duke's gift, helped increase the enrollment of women to fifty-four by 1904.

The major result of Duke's donation was its signal that the family had adopted Trinity College as the primary focus of its philanthropy. After the initial gift of $85,000 to attract the college to Durham, Duke had been shocked at the enormity of the financial needs of the school. During the severe economic depression of 1893 he is said to have claimed he wished he had never put a dollar in the

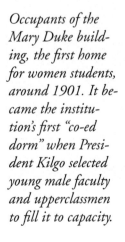

Occupants of the Mary Duke building, the first home for women students, around 1901. It became the institution's first "co-ed dorm" when President Kilgo selected young male faculty and upperclassmen to fill it to capacity.

college and that he would give no more. However, he followed the 1896 gift with two more in 1898 and 1900, each of $100,000. These donations, along with those of his sons, placed Trinity in greater financial shape than anyone dared dream at the time of the relocation of the college a decade earlier. To place the Duke family support in perspective, the total income for the University of North Carolina in 1899–1900 was only $48,000—$25,000 of which was a legislative appropriation.

On April 20, 1903, Washington Duke sent another of his infrequent letters to the board of trustees. This time no gift transpired. Instead he referred to his donation in 1896 with its restriction and wrote as follows: "I was then, and am still, interested in the higher education of the young women of the South; however, this is the only gift which I have ever made which in any way affects your policies in the management of the college. I now wish, and do hereby remove the conditions attached to this donation." By this letter he desired to remove any personally imposed restraints upon the board of trustees. Nevertheless, he thanked the board for accepting and complying with his interest in educating women.

Washington Duke's twin thrusts of confidence in Trinity and interest in the higher education of women helped propel the liberal arts college toward real leadership in the educational world and eventual university status.

Benjamin Duke's Considerable Contributions Came in a Quiet Way

Benjamin Newton Duke, tobacco and textile entrepreneur and philanthropist, was the primary benefactor of Trinity College after it relocated to Durham in 1892. He also was the principal link between the Duke family and the college and university until his death in 1929. While his father and brother received extensive publicity for vital, substantial donations, "Mr. Ben," as he was affectionately known, quietly supported the growing institution in innumerable ways. His support was so reliable and crucial that administrators acknowledged that without his generosity Duke never could have become a major university. President William P. Few always emphasized that the university was built around a strong undergraduate college. "Mr. Ben's" benefactions built Trinity College. He not only contributed money for construction and endowment but he also donated funds for equipment, salaries, remodeling, landscaping, and simply for current expenses.

For all of Ben Duke's support, the most modest and retiring of the Duke brothers has only a single sign identifying his gifts on campus. The stone column to the right at the main entrance to East Campus has a plaque dated July 12, 1915, acknowledging that the granite wall circling the campus is a gift of B. N. Duke. To the average visitor, Benjamin N. Duke remains unknown since he has no public statue dominating the campus like that of his father on East or his brother on West.

Unfortunately, an accurate tally of Ben Duke's philanthropy to the college and university is impossible. The most complete accounting discovered to date is in an unlikely source, the published *Bulletin* of Trinity College which happened to list annual contributions as part of an historical section. However, this listing lacks consistency and overlooks behind-the-scenes donations. Nevertheless, it is revealing. At various times Ben Duke is credited with donations totaling $182,000 to the general fund, $156,500 to current expenses, and $443,696 to endowment. Specific dollar amounts adding up to $438,500 are identified for a gymnasium, Alspaugh and Southgate dormitories, athletic fields, new buildings, grading and improvements to the campus, and scientific apparatus. For three years beginning in 1893 he donated $50 per year for tuition for sixty students from North Carolina. This $9,000 total in scholarships was critical in attracting students to the school, then at a new location and at a time of national economic depression. Such aid may be seen as a precursor to the scholarship and loan fund set up in 1925 in memory of his son, Angier B. Duke.

Beginning in 1902 Ben Duke also pledged annual contributions of $6,000 for chairs in Political Economy, French, German, and Applied Math. In 1904, he pledged an annual contribution of $3,000, to be matched by James B. Duke, to support the new School of Law. His annual contributions were increased to $20,000 in 1909. He donated $5,000 for a John M. Flowers Lectureship in 1916.

No dollar figures are given but "Mr. Ben" is credited with donating the following buildings and improvements: Asbury and Lanier in 1898, Branson in 1899, Bivins in 1905, West Duke and East Duke in 1911 and 1912, the erection of the granite wall in 1915, and the remodeling of Crowell. He also purchased thirty-eight and one-half acres of additional land, gave a large six-plate electrostatic machine, and periodically donated books to the library.

The listing in the *Bulletin* contains $1,234,696 in identifiable donations to Trinity College by Ben Duke without including his annual contributions toward faculty support or the Law School or his help in the construction of six new buildings. Ben Duke's contributions to Trinity College simply cannot be calculated. In fact, perhaps his most far-reaching assistance is not even mentioned except in private correspondence. In 1896 Edwin Mims, the only professor of English, took a year's leave of absence. His temporary replacement was a young Harvard-educated professor named William P. Few. Few was so well liked that when Mims returned, President John C. Kilgo asked Ben Duke to pick up Few's salary so he could continue at Trinity. Few in turn became the first Dean of the College and Kilgo's successor as president. During his thirty-year tenure as president from 1910 to 1940, Few persuaded James B. Duke to assume the family's philanthropic role toward the college. This Duke did in a spectacular way, endowing a university to be named, at Few's insistence, Duke University. According to James B. Duke, the university is named in large measure in honor of his father, Washington Duke, his brother, Benjamin Newton Duke, and his sister, Mary.

After the announcement of the Duke Endowment in 1924 and James B. Duke's premature death in 1925, Ben Duke was besieged with requests for money. Though confined to his home in New York due to illness, he continued his quiet philanthropy. Between 1926 and 1929 he donated approximately $3,000,000 to twenty-seven different southern institutions of higher education. One may frequently discover a building named for B. N. Duke on a private college campus such as nearby Elon College or at Lincoln Memorial University in Harrogate, Tennessee.

Today the Duke University community pays homage to Benjamin Duke through the B. N. Duke Memorial Organ, Flentrop 1976 in the Duke Chapel, and through the prestigious B. N. Duke Scholars program.

Benjamin Newton Duke (1855–1929) served on the college and university board of trustees for forty years, the longest tenure of any member of the Duke family.

Fiery John C. Kilgo Moved Trinity College Forward

President John C. Kilgo (1861–1922) won renewed support for the college after tumultuous times and the economic depression of the early 1890s.

John Carlisle Kilgo arrived on campus in August, 1894, as Trinity's fourth president, the second to lead the school since it relocated to Durham. Thirty-three years of age, he already had a reputation in Methodist circles as a committed churchman, fiery orator, and up and coming educator. Kilgo caught the attention of the search committee at Trinity College because of his success as the financial agent for Wofford College, a Methodist school in Spartanburg, South Carolina. There his charge was to increase endowment and awaken greater interest in the school, similar needs of Trinity. In 1894, when President John F. Crowell resigned, Trinity was heavily in debt because of the relocation, and dependent on annual donations by the Duke family which was thought to be disillusioned by the surprisingly large financial needs of the college.

A man of strong convictions and considerable oratorical skill, Kilgo was not timid, seeming almost to welcome a fight. His brother once commented that he doubted if Kilgo "ever preached a sermon or delivered an educational address that did not result in dividing the crowd....The pulpit was his throne, the privilege to occupy it his delight." He was in sharp contrast to his predecessor. Crowell had been intellectual, scholarly, more given to articulating a vision. Kilgo was passionate, and determined with a mixture of the idealistic and the practical. As preacher-president he led by idealism and accomplishment. His leadership drove the school forward and kept it forever in the public spotlight.

The students quickly became enamored with their youthful president. They identified with him as he sometimes walked about campus in shirtsleeves and cowboy hat with his dog alongside, and they appreciated his personal interest in their welfare. They also took pride in his leadership in erecting a flagpole for the nation's flag which some claimed to be the first flagpole on a college campus in the state. Today such a claim seems surely in error but in 1898 the nationalism fostered by the Spanish-American War competed with lingering recovery from, and a renewed interest in, the Civil War. Kilgo clearly preferred looking forward to backward.

Most students actually looked forward to the daily chapel services because of Kilgo's captivating oratory and his habit of inviting speakers to campus. However, he took a particularly bold step in 1896 when he invited the renowned African American leader, Booker T. Washington, to speak at Trinity when Washington was in town for another occasion. Students heartily welcomed Washington at his first appearance on a non-Black college campus in the south. Kilgo also spoke out forcefully for private, especially Christian, higher education and for the co-education of women and men. While his positions on these controversial issues aroused opposition and branded Trinity as clearly liberal for the day, they won strong favor with the Duke family. By 1902 Washington Duke had contributed $300,000 toward endowment, and his sons, Benjamin Newton and James Buchanan, had donated money for as varied causes as buildings, beautification, scholarships, faculty salaries and books for the new library.

Two legacies from the Kilgo era are an emphasis on high academic standards and a firm belief in academic freedom. Kilgo led Trinity in joining with five other institutions in founding the Association of Colleges and Preparatory Schools of the Southern States, an accrediting agency supporting high admission standards among member schools. Such a pledge, at a time when public schools, especially urban graded schools, were developing in the south, marked Trinity as being more committed to the quality of students than quantity. Trinity even started its own preparatory school, Trinity Park School, in order to prepare students for admission to the college.

In 1903, Kilgo eloquently defended Professor John Spencer Bassett before the Board of Trustees when state political leadership demanded that the history professor be fired for his questioning of the racial status quo which sought to keep the African Americans in subjugation. The president along with every faculty member was prepared to resign if the Board of Trustees acceded to the demands to fire Bassett. Their resignations were not offered, however, when the Board voted 18–7 to support Bassett's right to express his personal views.

Kilgo's presidential term of sixteen years is third in the history of the institution behind only the tenure of Braxton Craven from 1842 to 1882 and William P. Few from 1910 to 1940. When Kilgo resigned in 1910 upon election as Bishop in the Methodist Episcopal Church, South, the trustees voted to build a residence for him on campus. Today his house is used by the program of Continuing Education and is appropriately called Bishop's House. Another evident legacy of the era is the plaque in the main quadrangle of West Campus citing the aims of the university. The aims cast in bronze were written by President Kilgo in 1903 and continued by action of the Board of Trustees when Trinity College became Duke University in 1924.

Kilgo's personality and actions won friends and made enemies for Trinity College. One student remarked on being warned by his pastor to avoid the "strange fire" being offered at the school but most students and alumni were grateful for Kilgo's "bold attacks on the narrow tenets of orthodoxy" of the day. The "prince of pulpiteers" was recognized by the Board of Trustees as the "real builder of new Trinity." All were confident that the school was in a very strong position to become a leader in higher education in the twentieth century.

Kilgo's informality about campus, oratory and unconventional leadership style captured the loyalty of students.

The Day Booker T. Washington Came to Address Trinity College

In years past Trinity College had required Chapel services for all students twice a week. When John C. Kilgo was president from 1894 to 1910 he personally conducted the Chapel exercises. The compulsory nature undoubtedly dulled student interest, although one young man reluctantly admitted that Kilgo's superb oratory and penchant to invite surprise guests often made attendance worthwhile.

When the Durham County Colored Fair opened for its annual October run in 1896 few were surprised that Kilgo was invited to give the opening speech. As an idealistic yet activist churchman, it was not out of character for him to speak before predominantly black audiences. But it was surprising for him, with faculty

Booker T. Washington, founder of Tuskegee Institute and author of Up From Slavery, *was the most renowned African American leader of his day.*

approval, to suspend college classes for half a day so students could attend the Colored Fair. The reason was not Kilgo's opening remarks but those of the featured speaker, the renowned African American leader of the day, Booker T. Washington. Even more surprising and unprecedented was Kilgo's invitation to Washington to speak at Chapel exercises on the Trinity campus while he was in town. Washington thought enough of the invitation to write in his acclaimed autobiography, *Up From Slavery*, "It has been my privilege to deliver addresses at many of our leading colleges including Harvard, Yale, Williams, Amherst, Fisk, the University of Pennsylvania, Wellesley, the University of Michigan, Trinity College in North Carolina, and many more." Why did he include Trinity College in his list? Because Trinity was the first white institution of higher education in the south to extend Washington an invitation to speak on its campus.

Unfortunately neither the local nor the state press reported on the speech on campus. Washington's invitation and reception, however, was reported by the national progressive weekly magazine, *Outlook*. It noted that Washington's speech was received with "marked enthusiasm" and that his entourage of a half-dozen colleagues was treated with the "greatest courtesy" even receiving a "hearty college yell" by the students as they departed the campus.

The only campus publication of the day, the Trinity *Archive*, reported on Washington's visit in its November issue. Even though the contents of his speeches were not covered, his appearance obviously impressed the students. Washington's sincerity, devotion, simple bearing, and honest and conscientious service to his people elicited admiration. The editor concluded his comments saying, "We are glad that our college community gave him the welcome and hearing that is due to all truth from whatever source it may come."

Apparently Washington never forgot his reception at Trinity. Eight years later he proudly wrote alumnus Walter Hines Page that Trinity students had sought a conversation with him aboard the train on his most recent trip north. Even though Washington's visit was not widely publicized, it remains significant in the history of Trinity and Duke. It shows that the celebrated case of academic freedom, the Bassett Affair in 1903, was not without precedent. In the words of Louis R. Harlan, Washington's biographer and editor of his published papers, "The speech on campus in 1896 reveals that the college trustees' defense of Professor John Spencer Bassett was rooted in an atmosphere of comparative racial liberalism at Trinity College all through the Kilgo era."

Trinity Park High School: Duke's Preparatory School

The question of what constitutes a college seems anachronistic today but in an age of little standardization the answer had unpredictable ramifications. Trinity College proudly led in the battle for high standards in educational reform at the turn of the century. However, the operation of its own preparatory school was perhaps an unintended outcome of that leadership.

Around 1900 some "colleges" offered more college preparatory classes than true college level courses. More often than not, colleges admitted students with little regard to the quality of their secondary training and without entrance examinations. Not surprisingly, the disparity between an entering class and a graduating class was enormous. At Trinity, President John F. Crowell had begun to set the college above the norm as early as 1890 by abolishing all preparatory classes. Hence in 1895, when Chancellor Kirkland of Vanderbilt University issued a call for a meeting of institutions of higher education to discuss standardization, Trinity quickly responded. Along with five other schools Trinity College became a founding member of the resulting Association of Colleges and Preparatory Schools for the Southern States. The Association's members agreed upon a clear distinction between preparatory and college work as well as upon higher standardized admission requirements. Given the state of Southern public education, the member schools gambled on quality because they raised their entrance requirements above the capability of many of the just then developing high schools.

Asbury, the main building of Trinity Park School, was near the Alumni Memorial Gymnasium on East Campus. It was torn down in 1974 as a part of the redesign of the area at the time of the construction of the Mary Duke Biddle Music building.

President John C. Kilgo, Crowell's successor in 1894, continued to favor quality over quantity and profess an indifference to "mere numbers." Kilgo was not upset with a lack of increase in Trinity's enrollment in the wake of implementing the adopted standards of the new accrediting association. The Board of Trustees, however, was more concerned.

When Trinity College left Randolph County, the Methodist Church continued to support a preparatory school at the old campus. That school, and other Methodist schools designed to "feed" Trinity and satisfy local constituencies, struggled mightily to survive. Taking a political gamble of permanently alienating support in the western part of the state where "old Trinity" and its preparatory school were located, the Trinity Board of Trustees approved the creation of a preparatory school on campus. An anonymous donor, most assuredly Ben Duke, gave $12,500 to launch Trinity Park High School which was located in the northwest corner of the Durham campus. Bivins Building is the only remaining original building of the Trinity Park campus. Branson continues an original name but the theater is a different building on the same site.

Trinity Park or the Park School, as it was popularly known, became an instant success. Modeled after northern academies, its curriculum was designed to meet admissions at better colleges. It was no secret, however, that it was a "cram school" for Trinity College. When numerous Park School graduates organized their own social club at the University of North Carolina, in part to attract additional alumni, a Trinity official thought it quite "unbecoming."

Despite its quick organization over the summer, the prep school enrolled 72 students when it opened in the Fall of 1898. Thirty-eight percent of the students

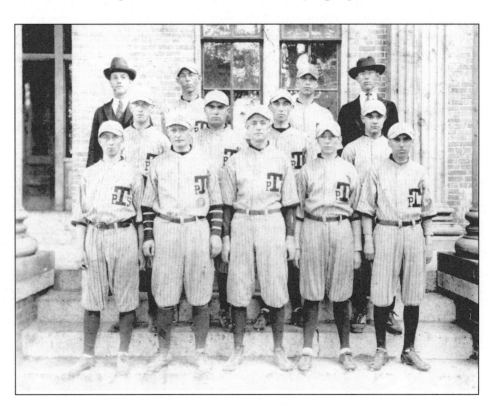

An undated photograph of a Trinity Park High School baseball team.

were from Durham and fourteen percent were young women, both percentages which remained significant throughout the history of the school. Enrollment increased to 161 the second year and before long the school actually generated surplus income. The focal point of the campus was the three-story brick Asbury Building which contained six classrooms, ladies' parlors, offices, two literary society meeting rooms and a chapel, library and study hall. Asbury was later used by the School of Engineering and the Music Department before being torn down in 1974 when the Mary Duke Biddle Music Building was constructed.

The stated aims of the school were to nourish character, stimulate intellect and promote good manners. The curriculum was organized into classical, Latin-scientific, and business programs. No music was taught in order to emphasize that it was in no way a traditional "finishing school." However, the advantage of attending concerts, plays and hearing speakers of national renown on the college campus was touted as a major asset. Park School students benefited greatly in their proximity to Trinity since they had access to the college library and athletic facilities. A medical fee also provided for room, board and nursing care at nearby Watts Hospital if necessary.

Trinity Park School was a resounding success although in reality daily life did not always measure up to publicity. For example, Branson boys lamented over having to sprint twenty yards to Asbury Building for shower facilities. Despite providing board, many students preferred to eat in boarding houses conveniently across Markham street both for their family atmosphere and good food.

The major measure of success was that ninety percent of the prep school graduates went on to college with the largest number attending Trinity. In turn, because of the admission of better students, President Kilgo boasted of a forty percent higher graduation rate at Trinity with twenty-five percent of its graduates going on for additional advanced academic work. Trinity Park School contributed significantly to the growing reputation of Trinity College and to its success in implementing higher collegiate standards. As the college became well known, attracting students from a much larger geographic area, pressures arose for additional facilities. Confronted with increased post-World War I enrollments, Trinity abolished the Park School in 1922. By then Southern public schools, especially urban high schools, could better prepare students for college admission. It is noteworthy that Duke University's acclaimed Talent Identification Program, also located on East Campus, is in some respects heir to the tradition of Trinity Park School.

Trick Photography "a-head" of Its Time _____

In the last quarter of the nineteenth century, rapid technological advances popularized photography. Publications such as Edward L. Wilson's *Cyclopaedic Photography: A Complete Handbook of the Terms, Processes, Formulae and Appliances Available in Photography*, published in 1894, explained new procedures for anyone willing to invest time and money. Trick photography, or in Wilson's terminology "double-pose or freak photography," became a fad. One practitioner, Professor M. H. Lockwood, left examples of his work in various collections in Perkins Library. As Professor of Physics and Biology from 1894 to 1897, Lockwood was part of the expansion of the faculty when Trinity College relocated to Durham. The "Before and After" images at mealtime are believed to be of Lockwood himself while the chess players are all Jerome Dowd, Professor of Economy and Social Science.

Narrow Walkway Names "The Ark"

In an out-of-the-way place on East Campus stands an historic century-old building with a most unusual name. A hand-painted Biblical scene over the door identifies the building as "The Ark," but such a designation raises more questions than answers. Built and furnished in 1898 with a donation from Benjamin N. Duke, the building was officially named the Angier B. Duke Gymnasium in honor of his son who was then fourteen years old. When the more modern Alumni Memorial Gymnasium opened across campus in 1923, the original gym assumed a new identity. Over the next decade as the building was put to a variety of uses, its long narrow bridge-like walkway forced people to enter "two by two"; hence, it became commonly referred to as the Ark.

The long walkway had been a gateway to a race track which was on the site when it was the Durham county fairgrounds. The Ark itself is built from lumber salvaged from the grandstand which was demolished when the fairground was donated for the site for Trinity College.

The building is probably the first college gymnasium in the state. The director of the gymnasium from 1899 to 1902, Albert Whitehouse, was the first paid

When built in 1898, campus literature claimed the new gymnasium to be the most complete building for physical education in the state.

physical education director in North Carolina. Whitehouse proudly boasted of a large and well-arranged building equipped with the latest gymnastic equipment, a running track, baseball batting cage, bowling alley, swimming pool, trophy room and shower baths. Formal instruction in physical education took place between Thanksgiving and Easter with outdoor activities scheduled in the fall and spring.

For years campus literature has proclaimed that the Ark was the site of the first intercollegiate basketball game in the state. On March 2, 1906, Trinity played host to Wake Forest in a game which Wake won 24 to 10. When Trinity made plans for the game it may have been the first scheduled. However, the gym had to be converted for basketball, a team had to be recruited and trained, and exams had to be completed. By the time the game took place, Wake Forest already had played Guilford College. However, it remains the first so-called "Big Four" basketball game as nearby schools—Duke, Carolina, State and Wake Forest— developed intense athletic rivalries.

No longer needed as a gym, the Ark became the cafeteria for men in 1923. The women had their own cafeteria in their new Southgate dormitory. When the new Union opened in 1930, the Ark became the campus laundry.

When West Campus opened and the original campus became exclusively for women, the students felt the need for a social center for relaxation and dancing. Though convenient to downtown, many students had to remain on campus due to financial constraints caused by the Great Depression. The Social Standards Committee of the Woman's Student Government and individual classes set about to renovate the Ark. They purchased curtains for thirty-six windows, wicker furniture, a piano, and ping-pong and bridge tables. One class spent $175 for a com-

Originally named the Angier B. Duke Gymnasium, the building has been popularly known as "The Ark" since the 1920s.

bination radio and victrola and all four of the classes in residence contributed toward refinishing the floor so one could dance in socks without worrying about splinters. The student bands so popular in the West Campus Union Ballroom performed in the Ark every Saturday night and one Wednesday evening per month. Les Brown, Class of 1936 and longtime director of the well known "Band of Renown," began his career in entertainment with one of the student bands that played regularly in the Ark. The Ark became a popular campus meeting place. As the *Chronicle* reported "Its past was noble; its present is enduring. Who can predict its future?"

The building continues in its eclectic tradition. It is primarily used by the Duke Dance Program and the American Dance Festival. On occasion in the summer it has had a snack bar—called the Barre—for dance festival participants. The undergraduate Duke Photo Group has its darkroom in the building. Few buildings on campus have had such a varied and student-centered history.

Foundations of the University Evident in Kilgo's Report to the Trustees in 1900 _____

The well-documented move of Trinity College to Durham includes an understanding of the hard times caused by the dramatic change and unexpected national economic depression. How quickly the college rebounded and fulfilled the high expectations of the move is less well understood. President John C. Kilgo devoted his annual report to the Board of Trustees in 1900 to a retrospective view of the development of the college during the 1890s. His report is a most interesting document in the history of Duke University.

Kilgo began by characterizing Crowell's administration as "a reformation under adverse circumstances" but "a signal success." He noted that Trinity's transformation of place and spirit helped reform Southern higher education. He was thankful for such a foundation when he became president in September, 1894.

By the turn of the century the physical changes were dramatic and easily observable. The number of buildings increased from 10 to 20 with those devoted to teaching purposes increasing from 2 to 11. Every addition was a cause for pride.

James B. Duke's first donation to the college was money to build a new library which was under construction at the time of Kilgo's report in 1900. Duke also gave $10,000 for new books.

The Scientific Building had 8 new labs, (4 in physics, 3 in chemistry and 1 in biology), with $13,000 worth of carefully selected apparatus. A gymnasium was added to support a physical education program for the expressed purpose of the total development of all students. Kilgo also noted the great amount of effort and expenditure in grading, paving and beautifying the ever increasing campus grounds. In total, the valuation of the buildings increased from $200,000 in 1895 to $725,000 in 1900. Almost single-handedly, Washington Duke's donations increased endowment from $22,500 to $333,750, possibly the second largest endowment of a private Southern college.

A new library, under construction in 1900, met the greatest need. In Randolph County, President Crowell took the significant step of merging the libraries of rival literary societies into a single college collection. In Durham, John Spencer Bassett, Professor of History and Manager of the Library, led the faculty in making the library the center of all academic activity. President Kilgo, believing the library to be the "one measure of the future development of the college," persuaded James B. Duke to make his first donation to Trinity a library building plus $10,000 for books. Even though the current holdings were only 15,000 books, the new library was constructed with a capacity of 100,000 volumes. Within eight years Trinity clearly emerged as one of the regions outstanding colleges in physical plant and endowment.

Kilgo knew the reputation of the college rested upon the quality of students and faculty. One of the most significant initiatives was to radically increase entrance requirements and remove college preparatory instruction from the respon-

The biology laboratory was one of eight new labs in the Crowell Science building in 1900.

sibility of Trinity's faculty. Consequently, a secondary preparatory school, Trinity Park School, was opened on the northwest corner of the campus. This risky move resulted in a drop in college enrollment but it clearly established high academic standards. It also greatly increased the percentage of college matriculants who graduated. Of great importance, it positioned Trinity College as a leader in formulating standards for accreditation in both secondary and higher education. It was clear that Trinity's commitment to quality was not mere lip service when it became a founding member of the Association of Colleges and Preparatory Schools of the Southern States.

When Kilgo became president the faculty numbered nine. By 1900 there were 29 faculty, 23 in the college and 6 in the preparatory school. Their training came from 15 different schools as varied as Tulane, the U.S. Naval Academy, Harvard, Cornell, Kansas, Johns Hopkins, and Leipzig. Neither did the faculty have a desire to retreat to an ivory tower. Trinity Faculty Lecture Series were begun in Charlotte, N.C. and in Saint Joseph's African Methodist Episcopal Church in Durham. Kilgo, himself, had spoken on education in 69 of the 97 counties in the state by 1900.

Trinity also eliminated the undergraduate Ph.B. degree, believing it to be substandard. In graduate work residency and specific course requirements were added to upgrade the M.A. degree. Graduate enrollment increased from 1 to 18 prompting Kilgo to say "no other single change in the college promises better results."

In conclusion Kilgo noted that there was no more gratifying indication of the spirit of the college than that over six years, 25 percent of the graduates were enrolled in or arranging additional education. By vocation, the graduates during his tenure to date numbered 34 teachers, 23 preachers, 15 businessmen, 10 graduate students, 7 doctors, 7 lawyers, 2 electrical engineers, 2 farmers, and 1 each in architecture, manufacturing and government employment.

Kilgo believed the character and spirit of the college to be grounded in individual personal faith, a strong belief in freedom, service to mankind, high standards, and loyalty. These ideals represented the fruition of the labors of Braxton Craven and John F. Crowell, and the foundation of future decisions by William P. Few and his successors. By 1900, even before the famous Bassett Affair affirming academic freedom, a clear foundation was set for later milestones such as Rhodes Scholars, a Phi Beta Kappa chapter, and even university status.

Honoring Founders a Tradition Since 1901

One of the long-standing traditions of Trinity College and Duke University is the observance of honoring the benefactors of the institution. The practice was formalized by the Board of Trustees on June 4, 1901, when October 3 was designated as Benefactors' Day in honor of Washington Duke. The annual college holiday came about in response to Duke's gift of $100,000 for endowment which raised his donations to Trinity College to $444,250, a sum then unparalleled in the South. The first official observance in October, 1901, was a joyous affair. With Washington Duke sitting on the stage, the program consisted of music by a Durham chorus and a Raleigh orchestra, an address by Bishop Hendrix of Missouri, and the reading of the gifts to the college received during the year. Hearty student cheers resounded after the reading of each gift. The date selected for the observance was the birthday of Duke's grandson, George Washington Duke, son of Benjamin and Sarah Duke, who died in early childhood.

Tree planting ceremonies were a traditional part of Founders' Day celebrations for decades. Here senior class officers assist in beautifying East Campus in 1946.

The original intent "to honor Washington Duke forever" has been kept in spirit but through the years the name and even date of the annual observance has changed. It has been called Benefactors' Day (1901–1924), Duke University Day (1926–1947), and since 1948, Founders' Day. The most common forms of recognition have been an address on campus, the laying of a wreath at the tombs of the Dukes, and for many years the planting of trees by the senior class presidents to beautify the campus. The day has been the occasion for the presentation of special donations and awards, the dedication of buildings or gifts such as the Flentrop Organ in 1976, and the awarding of honorary degrees. The most elaborate celebrations occurred in the year-long Centennial Celebration of 1938–1939, and on the 100th Anniversary of James B. Duke's birth in 1956. Although the announcement of the selection of four presidents has been made at trustees meetings on Founders' Day weekend, only President Douglas M. Knight has been inaugurated as part of the annual celebration.

After the creation of Duke University, the date shifted to December 11 in honor of the signing of the Indenture of The Duke Endowment. A more accurate date perhaps would have been December 29 when the trustees met, accepted the terms of the Indenture, and changed the name of the college to Duke University, but that date was totally inappropriate for a campus celebration. The new Duke University Day was largely a product of the Office of Alumni Affairs. Local alumni chapters were encouraged to meet on December 11 to elect officers and to hear what could be characterized as a "state of the university" report. These meetings grew from ten in North Carolina and Virginia in 1926 to a high of over sixty nationwide in 1936. In 1927 the first meeting was held in New York City, and in 1930 the first Alumni chapter was organized in Los Angeles. In 1931 there also were observances in China and Japan. These meetings were greatly curtailed from 1939 to 1945.

After 1948 primary attention returned to campus where prominent speakers were featured along with significant announcements to the University community. Major gifts or grants were announced from the Rockefeller Foundation in 1949, the Ford Foundation in 1955, and The Duke Endowment in 1952 and 1957.

In 1967 the annual event was shifted to the Sunday nearest December 11 with the primary focus on the morning worship service in the Chapel. In 1986 that observance was extended to a long weekend beginning with a formal campus-wide Convocation on Thursday immediately following an annual meeting of the faculty. This focus, again on a Convocation, meets the long-felt desire that the celebration be a time when students and faculty of all the schools, and administrators, staff, and friends of the university can come together as one in common appreciation of the past and future of Duke University. Since the weekend always includes a quarterly meeting of the board of trustees and, since 1980, hosts the Founders' Society as well, it truly marks a high point in the academic year of the university. In 1997 Founders' recognition returned to a fall weekend close to the original 1901 October date. Since the major realignment of the academic calendar, the December date always fell on reading day or the first day of exams, an inauspicious time to attract students or faculty to an official convocation.

John Spencer Bassett's Contribution More Than a Stand for Academic Freedom

Trinity College's most renowned professor is fondly remembered on campus but hardly in a fashion that recognizes the totality of his accomplishments. When John Spencer Bassett is mentioned it is almost always in reference to the Bassett Affair in 1903, the cornerstone of the university's policy of academic freedom, which was, indeed, a significant event in the evolution of academic freedom in the history of higher education. But while of great significance, dwelling on that incident does little to reveal the personality and accomplishments of the man who would be a strong candidate in a debate on the most influential faculty member in the history of the institution.

Born in rural eastern North Carolina in 1867 amid the poverty of a defeated South, Bassett had intermittent schooling until his devoutly Methodist parents sent him to their church's college, Trinity, then in Randolph County. Entering as a junior in 1886 he experienced the arrival of a new president, John F. Crowell, for his senior year. Crowell came from the North unencumbered by southern tra-

The Trinity faculty in 1891. John Spencer Bassett is standing on the left, second row.

dition and prejudices and full of zeal for educational reform. Bassett, infused with the excitement of research in original sources and with a broadened perspective learned in the new courses of sociology and economics introduced by Crowell, graduated with a degree in history. He began teaching in the public schools of Durham but soon headed north to Johns Hopkins University to earn a Ph.D. degree in history in the famous seminar of Herbert Baxter Adams. Bassett returned after Trinity relocated to Durham but this time with the best education then available in his field and as professor of history at his alma mater. Of Adams, Bassett later wrote, "You have been to me more than an instructor. You have given me sparks of yourself, and you have made me hope that I might be a useful man in some not unimportant way."

At Trinity Bassett was a very popular teacher who had the willingness to work hard and the discipline to balance his teaching with his primary love of research and writing. Yet his devotion to his students was legendary. When tragedy struck in one family a student's aunt implored Bassett to comfort the young man because her nephew had spoken of his great admiration for his professor. Another student made an intriguing comment about Bassett, writing, "He is the one faculty member who believes that Jesus Christ died for freshmen too."

Bassett did not hesitate to take on responsibilities outside the classroom. He revitalized the Trinity College Historical Society which had been founded by his predecessor, Stephen B. Weeks, to foster the study of southern history. Bassett opened an historical museum, turning the entire college community into collectors in the process. Believing that everyone could collect, if not write, his ulterior motive was to acquire a body of materials for historical research. Students, administrators, and alumni combed their attics donating Confederate money, Indian relics, travel souvenirs, and political memorabilia as well as volumes of books, pamphlets, religious and secular newspapers, maps, and manuscripts. After a few years Bassett proudly reported to Adams that over 2,000 documents had been collected for use in primary research. Soon "manager of the library" was added to his varied duties.

In 1906 an analysis of the historical society's meetings revealed that presentations had been made by 53 students, 38 faculty and 6 visiting scholars. Following the Johns Hopkins example of a series of published research, Bassett began an annual publication of *Historical Papers* of the Trinity society in 1897. At first a cheaply reproduced set of reprints of student articles from the campus magazine, *The Archive,* the series became more sophisticated and widely distributed when the administration enthusiastically endorsed it. Some noteworthy early articles were on the Ku Klux Klan, the North Carolina Manumission Society, and William W. Holden, the Governor of North Carolina during Reconstruction. Bassett proudly wrote Adams, "So far as I know, this is but one of three [academic] historical publications in the South. It is the only one in North Carolina."

Museum of the Trinity College Historical Society. Bassett used the excitement generated by collecting artifacts to also collect research materials for the library.

The society also sponsored an annual patriotic town-gown civic rally intentionally set on February 22, the birth of George Washington, and not on a date commemorating a Confederate hero. Of the historical society, a respected historian later wrote, "There is reason to believe no local historical association ever succeeded better than the Society at Trinity College in effecting its program."

In yet another corollary to his passion for learning, Bassett launched a secret student honor society based on academic distinction and service in 1890. Named "9019," presumably because nineteen qualifying members had averages of above ninety, the society was a precursor to Phi Beta Kappa which was chartered in 1920.

Surprisingly these extracurricular endeavors were carried on despite a teaching load of fifteen and sometimes eighteen hours a semester. Growing slowly in its early years in Durham, Trinity did not have the means to support more than a single faculty member per discipline. Having to teach history courses far afield of his primary interests, Bassett once privately lamented over the continuance of a "troublesome" French history class. Intermittently he introduced new courses such as a senior seminar in Contemporary History which emphasized class reports with special attention to Southern development. Another course, the History of North Carolina, offered students a chance "to learn methods of original research and to gain an impetus to historical writing and the collection of historical materials."

Extremely popular on campus and confident in his ability which was earning accolades in the region and nation, Bassett, nevertheless, had periodic misgivings about life at Trinity and in his native South. He believed his salary to be inadequate for growing family responsibilities and the teaching load constantly interfered with time for research and writing. He also became exasperated at the slow pace of change in the region. Seeking a wider audience than a single college campus, he successfully launched a journal of thought and action, the *South Atlantic Quarterly*, in 1902. An editorial in that journal and the resulting clamor for his dismissal from the college faculty by Democratic political leaders in the state, rudely altered the comfortable position he had attained at Trinity. In 1896, he had written Adams, "There are a lot of fools in N. C. and it takes some time to lick them into shape.... Trinity is about the only place in the state that is trying to do it [but]...as long as the fool-killing is to go on I want to be here to see the fun." Unfortunately John Spencer Bassett became among the hunted.

[This article is based in part on "John Spencer Bassett as a Historian of the South" by Wendell H. Stephenson, *North Carolina Historical Review*, July, 1948.]

John Spencer Bassett:
The Reform Impulse Versus the Scholar _____

John Spencer Bassett, clearly one of the hardest working and most respected men at Trinity, quickly earned regional and national renown as well. Yet his lasting significance is perhaps more as a promoter of historical scholarship than author. His interests were so varied he did not leave a lasting interpretative theme upon a single subject of American history nor did he have the opportunity to train a group of graduate students in a particular methodology. His forte was in inspiring individuals to question orthodoxy and seek "truth." His vehicle was the "new history" based on original research in primary sources. He was a significant promoter of collecting historical materials as well as an accomplished practitioner in using a variety of sources in interpreting the past. Like many southern intellectuals of his era, he found it difficult to balance an impulse for reform with his scholarly training. He began with the South as his primary laboratory but he moved on to more national themes as his scholarship matured and he moved to New England to live.

At the beginning of the 1897–98 academic year Bassett examined the status of history in the South and revealed a bit of his philosophy in an address to the Trinity College Historical Society. In outline he discussed three summary statements: 1) there is a loose idea of what shall be good history, 2) there is little understanding about the proper training of those who write history, and 3) there is a lack of system or attention in the collection of historical documents. Good history, to Bassett, was not the all-too-common ancestor worship, simple preservation of anecdotes, or self-serving memoir. It was instead a faithful, systematic, comprehensive record of our heritage. In short, it was serious, hard work. He insisted that the practice of history should be left to trained professionals who

Volume II.   OCTOBER, 1903.   Number 4.

The

South Atlantic Quarterly.

Stirring Up the Fires of Race Antipathy

Whatever be his view of the negro problem the average American knows that in the la[...] [...]rs there has been a notable increase in the general [...] [...]gro. This development has occurred in both [...] In the South it has manifested itself in[...] [...]e North. We see it there in restrictio[...] [...]assage of laws for "Jim Crow" car[...] [...]nching, and in a general augmen[...] [...]on on the part of Southerners to [...] [...]utrage." In the North it is seen[...] [...]e South, and it is especially n[...] [...] was supposed formerly not t[...] [...]occasional acts of violence, as [...] [...]d in a growing opinion which on[...] [...]and in private conversation with[...] [...]m in the North is most strongly held [...] [...]noteworthy that in most of the larg[...] [...] rapid increase of the negro population[...]

The causes of this [...] [...]ps numerous. But there are three facts [...] [...]ottom and which are worthy of special consideration. [...]ese are; inherent race antipathy, the progress of the negro himself, and the fact that the negro problem is, and has been for a long time, a political matter.

Race antipathy is as old as the negro's residence in America.

must weigh evidence, have a scientific spirit for facts, have knowledge of other places and times, and above all have a facility in coming to historical judgments. Hitting close to home, he believed that "in the South, the Confederate-Brigadier-General kind of an historian" was "a snake which ought to be hit whenever possible." Finally, pride and loyalty were not sufficient qualifications to write history. Original materials were vital to record and interpret the past.

Bassett practiced this philosophy by using a variety of resources like diaries, court reports, laws and codes, newspapers, and published colonial records to write numerous articles, monographs, textbooks, and edited works. His subjects ranged from colonial and ante-bellum North Carolina history to the League of Nations. His contribution to the American Nation Series, *The Federalist System, 1789–1801*, was highly praised as was his two-volume *Life of Andrew Jackson* and six edited volumes of the *Correspondence of Andrew Jackson*. An account of the Southern plantation overseer objectively revealed an aspect of the plantation system that had been overlooked in favor of attention to planters and slaves. In addition he encouraged others to publish by editing the *Trinity College Historical Papers* and founding the *South Atlantic Quarterly*, "a journal devoted to the literary, historical, and social development of the South."

Ironically, it is as a promoter of reform in a shift of emphasis from his professed ideal of scholarly objectivity for which John Spencer Bassett is best remembered. His primary purpose in founding the *South Atlantic Quarterly* at Trinity College in 1902 was to promote the "liberty to think." Patterned after the *Sewanee Review*, Bassett sought "sober and instructive articles" for the *South Atlantic Quarterly* to appeal to an "audience of serious minded southerners." He often wrote editorials on selected themes in certain quarterly issues. Given the times, a discussion of race was inevitable. Bassett did not shy away from the controversial topic. One of his articles, "Two Negro Leaders," was pathfinding. In it he contrasted the lives of Booker T. Washington and William E. B. DuBois, thus becoming one of the first scholars to appreciate the significance of the two schools of thought that emanated from their differing philosophies. In his thoughtful analysis Bassett said that there should be vocational education for the many, which was Washington's view, and that there should be cultural education for the few which was the view of DuBois. He also noted that there should be a sympathetic attitude on the part of white people toward Negro advancement in both directions. His views and thoughtful articles by others in the *South Atlantic Quarterly* were read and praised by southern liberals and northern scholars, but by-and-large ignored by most southerners, especially conservative leaders.

To gain attention, Bassett later admitted to doing a very unprofessional thing. With galley proofs of an editorial in hand, he inserted a sentence praising the life of Booker T. Washington and ranking him second in comparison to Robert E. Lee of southerners born in a hundred years. Such a sentiment invited controversy at a time when race baiting was commonplace due to the revival of bitter partisan politics with the division of the Democratic Party, the rise of the Populist third party, and revival of the Republican Party. State Democratic leaders in nearby Raleigh who were also represented on the Trinity College Board of Trustees demanded that Professor Bassett be fired. When the attack spread to the college and parents were urged to withdraw their children from school and churchmen were encouraged not to recommend the college to prospective students, Bassett offered his resignation. Lines clearly were drawn between a partisan Democratic press that blatantly referred to the historian as "Professor bASSett" who threatened the accepted "southern way of life" and between proponents of the then developing concept of academic freedom. On December 2, 1903, at about 3:00 a.m., the Trinity Board of Trustees voted 18 to 7 not to accept the resignation of Bassett. Jubilant students who had been listening to the debate through skylights and heating registers built bonfires and celebrated until dawn. It was later revealed that President Kilgo and the college faculty were prepared to resign if the trustees had voted to dismiss Bassett. A year later President Theodore Roosevelt spoke in Durham extolling Trinity's courageous stand for academic freedom.

Trinity basked in favorable publicity following what has come to be called the "Bassett Affair" and despite predictions to the contrary enrollment continued to increase. Rumors circulated almost immediately that Bassett would leave but he built an impressive new house, still standing at 410 N. Buchanan Boulevard, in part to prove otherwise. Nevertheless, when teaching offers materialized from Smith College and Yale University, he accepted the offer from Smith and moved to Northampton, Massachusetts in 1906. Bassett never commented publicly on his move but he alluded to several reasons in private correspondence. There was no question that he welcomed a reduced teaching load with increased time for research and writing. He also looked forward to living in New England. He confided to his Trinity colleague, William K. Boyd, that the South was too used to antiquarianism and arousement instead of history and scholarly thinking, a state, he believed, any cultured community ought to have long passed. He also tired of the tension he felt between his role as a scholar and the pull to be a reformer in a region he cared very much about. He concluded that he could not write history and direct public sentiment at the same time. His decided first choice was to write history. Bassett corresponded with numerous friends in the South throughout his life and he worked diligently to get southern topics included in meetings of professional associations. Living until 1928, he never lost his love for his native region, although he never regretted his move north either.

[This article is based in part on "The Negro in the Thinking and Writing of John Spencer Bassett" by Wendell H. Stephenson, *North Carolina Historical Review*, October, 1948. Bassett's papers have only recently been donated and opened for research at the Library of Congress in Washington, D.C. Heretofore, Stephenson is the only historian who has had access to his personal correspondence.]

"Cap" Card's "March Madness"

Duke sports fans have developed a special fondness for the early Spring. "March Madness" is peculiar to television and the NCAA and ACC tournaments, but intercollegiate basketball competition in the state began almost one hundred years ago with enthusiastic participation by Trinity College. The initiator at Trinity was Wilbur Wade "Cap" Card for whom Card Gymnasium is named. In 1906 basketball was a relatively new sport. It had been invented in 1891 by James Naismith, a YMCA director in Springfield, Massachusetts, who sought an indoor activity during the harsh New England winter. It spread more quickly through the YMCA movement than among colleges where football and baseball reigned supreme. Many thought the sport an "impracticable game" that would never attain popularity, especially in the south, but Trinity's Card advocated it. A native of nearby Franklinton, N. C., Card graduated from Trinity College in 1900, and upon choosing athletics for a career, sought the best training available in hygiene and physical education at Harvard University. After a year of academic study, he returned to Harvard every summer through 1913 to train and work at the famed

Coach Wilbur Wade "Cap" Card, for whom Card Gymnasium is named, appears in formal attire with the Trinity basketball team of 1906.

Sargent Normal School of Physical Education. While at his first job as director of the Mobile, Alabama YMCA, Card received an invitation from President John C. Kilgo to return to his alma mater as Director of a new program in physical education.

The college had an excellent new facility in the Angier B. Duke Gymnasium, now known as the Ark, and superb playing fields, complete with a grandstand from a previous race track, on its spacious campus. Card coached baseball and introduced gymnastics, track and field, hockey, bowling, fencing, swimming and volleyball to the campus. Not everyone, however, appreciated the new physical activity. One student successfully won exemption from required participation because he walked four miles round-trip at dawn every day to milk cows to earn money to attend school.

Ever since football was banned in 1895 students deplored the lack of intercollegiate competition. In late 1905, Richard Crozier, the coach at nearby Wake Forest College, approached Trinity for a basketball game. Card knew the game and was interested, but he had to convert the gym and recruit and train a team, neither of which could begin until after the semester's exams. By the time Trinity played host to Wake Forest on March 2, 1906, Wake and Guilford College had played the first intercollegiate game in the state, but the game in what is now the Ark on East Campus marked the beginning of so-called "Big Four" or Tobacco Road rivalry. Wake won the game 24–10 but the Trinity team was proud of its effort since it had trailed 18–3 at the half. No one from Trinity had ever played a game and a graduate student in English as well as a Law student had to be recruited even to make up a team.

The original game is hardly recognizable today. Two-handed passes and shots were the norm. The goal had a bottom to catch the ball which had to be knocked out with a stick after every score. A center jump began every quarter as well as play after every score, even free throws. A designated shooter attempted all a team's free throws. Few fouls were called, perhaps because the home team provided the umpire and the opposing coach was always the referee. Occasionally officials stopped the contest to consult the rule book.

Card, who coached the Trinity team for seven years, had a 30–17 record with a majority of the opponents being high school and YMCA teams. Gradually intercollegiate competition emerged with Wake Forest, Guilford, Davidson, William and Mary, VMI, VPI, Virginia, Tennessee, A & M (NCSU) and Furman. Trinity had the state's first twenty victory season with a 20–4 record in 1917. Surprisingly UNC did not join Trinity's schedule until 1922.

After Card, Trinity had a succession of ten coaches in fifteen years and it was not until the arrival of Edmund M. Cameron in 1929 that stability returned to the program. In Cameron's first year Duke helped launch the Southern Conference and, to the surprise of many, advanced to the tournament championship game. In Cameron's second year Duke had its first All-American player, Bill Werber, and the path to today's "March Madness" was set.

Duke's Most Impressive Inauguration

A look back at one of our most festive and significant inaugural ceremonies reminds us how important such occasions can be. An inauguration is a time of celebration and anticipation, a moment when an academic institution can affirm its past, define its purpose and interpret its role to a wider audience. The inauguration of President William P. Few on November 9, 1910, was such an auspicious occasion for Trinity College.

William Preston Few (1867–1940) at his inauguration as president in 1910.

In 1910 the school had existed for seventy-two years, eighteen of which had been in Durham. Despite annual support from the Duke family, financial problems always seemed close at hand. The college, nevertheless, was a growing, respected school earning a solid reputation. Trinity was a leader in the South in educational reform. It had welcomed the renowned African American leader Booker T. Washington to its campus in 1896. Nationally, it had won renown as well as praise from President Theodore Roosevelt in the celebrated case of academic freedom when the trustees stood by Professor John S. Bassett in 1903.

A change of presidents offered the opportunity to invite the nation's educational leadership to visit the campus, meet the new president and assess the reputation of the college. The small regional college clearly aroused curiosity among leaders in higher education. No less than forty-one percent of the official delegates who marched in the academic procession at the inaugural ceremony were college and university presidents who attended the ceremony themselves instead of appointing representatives. Delegates came from all sections of the country, large and small institutions, and schools for men and women. A special Pullman train, undoubtedly provided by Ben Duke, brought guests to Durham from the main east coast rail line through Greensboro. The day's festivities concluded with a tour of the city in automobiles provided by citizens of Durham and an elaborate reception at the home of Benjamin Duke.

On campus official ceremonies began with the dedication of the new West Duke Building, another magnificent gift of Ben Duke. The induction of the new president was marked by the presentation of the college charter and seal to William P. Few by John C. Kilgo, the retiring president and recently elected Methodist Bishop. Governor W. W. Kitchen of North Carolina and President Judson of the University of Chicago gave addresses of congratulations.

Though a Trinity faculty member for fourteen years and the college's only dean for eight, Few's inaugural address served as an important introduction. Soft-spoken, introspective and even shy in comparison to Kilgo, Few, a Shakespearean scholar, had gladly worked in the background on academic affairs at Trinity. Everyone looked forward to his inaugural address with anticipation.

Few began his address by stating it was appropriate to discuss the place of the college in southern history and to say plainly what Trinity College should undertake to do. The audience quickly grasped, however, that his style was to speak in carefully considered generalizations. He inspired the audience with eloquent yet quietly stated grand ideals not exhortation. The address stressed freedom, truth, the important evolving democratic experiment in government, courage both individual and institutional, and above all, service, religion and character. There was nothing narrow-minded or sectarian in his plan for Trinity and he offered a prescription for lasting success. Concluding, Few said "The greatness of a college depends not upon the size of its plant or the number of its students, but upon the quality of those who teach and the quality of those who learn, and upon its ideals and its influence."

The formal ceremony adjourned to an extravagant luncheon where Chancellor James H. Kirkland of Vanderbilt University presided as toastmaster. The published remarks clearly illustrate that all enjoyed themselves immensely. Speakers at the luncheon included President Abbott Lowell of Harvard University, Dean Andrew F. West of Princeton University, the Honorable Elmer E. Brown, Commissioner of Education, Dean John F. Downey of the University of Minnesota, Governor Kitchen of North Carolina, Dean Frederick Jones of Yale University and President Edwin Craighead of Tulane University.

The day marked a high point in the history of the college. Amid a gracious serving of southern hospitality, the new president and the college impressed everyone. Ben Duke later confided to a friend, "I felt prouder of Trinity than ever before. There were representatives here from leading colleges and universities in the United States, and they were as much astonished at what they saw and heard as they were pleased at the reception given them. It was a great day for not only Trinity and Duke, but for the entire state."

Letter at Graduation in 1912 Notes Value of a College Education

The institution now known as Duke University has been awarding degrees upon the completion of a prescribed course of study since the 1852–53 academic year. Thousands of students and their families have experienced the vivid emotions of the awarding of a college or university degree and passage into what is commonly referred by today's students as the "real world." Scores of commencement speakers have attempted to place a value on the student experience while challenging the graduates to use their hard-won knowledge to conquer the problems of the day.

While public ceremonies properly reflect collective joy, perhaps the true meaning behind graduation is more of an individual or family affair. A universal feeling is one of pride. Documentation of this sentiment is difficult to come by, especially as letter writing increasingly has become a lost art. The University Archives recently received a poignantly prideful letter written at graduation from Trinity College in 1912. At that time, graduation from college was a rare event. The vast majority of graduates, especially in the south, were the first members of

The class of 1912 on the steps of the library.

their family to earn diplomas, either from high school or college. The recipient of the letter was Edwin L. Jones from Charlotte, North Carolina, a member of Trinity's senior class who had won the Orator's Medal of the Hesperian Literary Society. He had mailed a copy of the notice of the award from the student newspaper, the *Chronicle*, to his parents along with the schedule of the commencement weekend. His father replied, expressing a universal sentiment not uncommon today. (The writer's evident limited education adds significantly to the personal importance of the occasion.)

"My Dear Son," the letter began. "I cant tell you how glad I was to know that you had won the metal[.] now you can see that God has give you a delivery of voice. it does my heart good to see that you are taking advantage of a opertunity that I diden have[.] I wanted Education when I was a boy. but I diden have the chance to get some. I am glad that you have made good at college[.] I have worked hard every sence I have ben a little boy. but I dont mind working hard as I have to get you through College[.] As I rid the a count in your little paper of you winning the metal, it repaid me for all that I have spent on your schooling[.] I & mama do want to get up for your gratuation but I dont see how both of us will get to go as the children is so small to leave by themselves. Good by, Your Papa."

Edwin L. Jones, Jr. made the most of his family's priceless gift of educational opportunity. The listing of activities under his senior portrait in the *Chanticleer*, the college yearbook, notes academic honors, varied literary society, Y.M.C.A. and debate activities, positions of responsibility on the *Chronicle's* business staff, letters in track and basketball, and membership in the highest campus honorary organization, "9019." Perhaps equally as important, Jones met, courted and later married classmate Annabel Lambeth, a Magna Cum Laude graduate with Honors in French, from Thomasville, North Carolina. Their marriage marks the beginning of generations of Duke graduates from the Jones family. Edwin L. Jones, Jr.'s later service on the Board of Trustees and generosity in support of his alma mater likewise inspired varied service and support throughout the university by numerous family members.

With the growth of higher education in the twentieth century, the earning of a college degree is sometimes taken for granted. Duke University, however, still has graduates who are the first members of their families to receive a degree. A university education remains an accomplishment of the highest order worthy of pride by parents and students alike.

The Sower: An Important Gift from James B. Duke

The Trinity *Chronicle* in November, 1914, announced that a bronze figure representing the Sower had recently been placed on campus as a gift of Mr. James B. Duke. Of all the statuary on campus, that of the Sower, observable on the lawn between the entrance to East Campus and the East Duke building, is the only one not depicting a member of the Duke family or faculty or an historical figure of the college or university. To the university community the statue's history is interesting, its part in campus tradition amusing, and its role enduring.

At the time of the gift, John C. Kilgo, former president of Trinity College (1894–1910), was residing on campus as a Bishop of the Methodist Episcopal Church, South. Kilgo was especially close to the Duke family and, while visiting James B. Duke, he admired the statue which was part of the extensive landscaping at Duke's estate in New Jersey. Duke promptly donated the Sower to Trinity College.

Kilgo was particularly drawn to the figure because of an inspiring, popular Baccalaureate sermon based on the parable of the sower from the Gospel of Matthew preached two years previously at Trinity commencement by his colleague Bishop W. T. McDowell. Kilgo also admired the statue's "strength and nobleness of face and the strong arm with which the laborer faced his daily toil." He believed the statue would be a powerful model for students as they completed four years of study and faced the challenge of life.

Duke had discovered the Sower while on a grand tour of Europe and purchased it in Leipzig. The *Chronicle* reported that the statue was signed by St. Walter but that no information was available about the sculptor. An inscription on the statue reveals that it was a production of the Gladenbeck Foundry in Freidrechshagen near

The Sower, a sculpture of a 17th-century peasant sowing in his field, was a gift of James B. Duke.

Berlin. Research has revealed that the sculptor was Stephan Anton Friedrich Walter, born in Nurnberg in 1871. A catalog from the Great Berlin Exhibition of Art in 1911 reveals that Walter had been an independent sculptor since 1898 and he first participated in the Berlin exhibition in 1899. Among his works was a figure entitled "Sower From The Time of the Great Elector." Thus the figure is that of a seventeenth-century peasant sowing his fields. The university statue is undoubtedly a small-scale version of the heroic size figure believed to have been made for the Neiderbariner Hospital in Berlin. Unfortunately, little else is known about Stephan Walter. A few additional works are noted and he is identified as a member of the Union of Berlin Artists in the 1928 edition of *Wer Ist's?*, the German version of *Who's Who*.

On campus, the statue assumed a role unanticipated by Bishop Kilgo. At a time when women students were permitted only three dates a week, and those were carefully defined, students could stroll about certain areas of campus without it counting as an allowed date. The Sower acquired the role of cupid as couples began placing pennies in his hand and claiming a kiss from their partner if the pennies were gone upon return. Although the origin of this practice is largely unknown, and it is unnecessary to most students today, it is not uncommon still to discover pennies in the Sower's hand.

Campus wags have had fun with the statue as well. Parents have characterized it as a student with a hand out for money, and a campus caretaker reportedly told visitors for years that it was a statue of Mr. Duke sowing his money. An incorrect oral tradition sometimes refers to the statue as Johnny Appleseed.

In 1980 at the urging of staff member Rebekah Kirby, the Founders' Society adopted the figure as its symbol. Franklin Creech, an alumnus of the class of 1964, has fashioned a remarkable replica of the Sower that is twelve inches high which the university presents to designated donors at the annual meeting of the Founders' Society on Founders' Day. The Founders' Society honors individuals who establish named, permanent, fully funded endowments thus providing for the future of Duke University. By reason of their generosity, these founders are sowing that future generations will reap the harvest of their labor.

The Sower maintains a unique position in the history of the university. First revered by Trinity College students, it became a special symbol for residents of the Woman's College when East Campus was exclusively for women. Now it has become a university symbol acknowledging the need and expressing gratitude for continuing, vital financial support.

President William P. Few's Career
Unparalleled at the University

On October 16, 1940, an extra edition of the *Chronicle* informed the university community of the death of President William Preston Few at age seventy-two. Few's forty-four-year career at Trinity College and Duke University is without parallel. He came in 1896 for one year to fill-in for a professor on leave. Few was so well liked that President John F. Kilgo appealed to Benjamin N. Duke to pay his salary so he could remain. English thereby became the first academic department to have a second professor. In 1902 Few became the first Dean of Trinity College, doubling the administration. When Kilgo was elected a Bishop in the Methodist Church in 1910, Few succeeded him as president. The students and faculty were delighted with the choice.

William Preston Few planned and launched the new university in his thirty-year tenure as president from 1910 to 1940.

As president for thirty years, Few presided over the transformation of Trinity College into Duke University. At his inauguration in 1910 the college had 363 students and 32 faculty. At his death Duke University had nine schools, 3,716 students, and 476 faculty. This growth of a small regional college into a nationally known university represented a greater transformation in a shorter period of time than had ever occurred in the South and perhaps in the nation.

One has to probe deeply in assessing the reasons for Few's spectacularly successful presidency. He easily could be underestimated at first impression. A typical reaction was recorded by a visiting official from Olmsted Associates, the renowned landscaping firm, when the new campus was being planned. His report to the home office praised several university officials but of Few he wrote, "He had little to say and seemed not a very forceful man."

Few led by the force of his commitment and by seizing opportunity and building upon success, not by dynamic personality. He was a complex man, difficult to describe although

Professor Robert H. Woody has written a thought-provoking, sensitive biographical appreciation. In Woody's phraseology, Few was slight of build with a certain gauntness. To some he had an almost "Lincolnesque" appeal. He had large, luminous brown eyes, capable of a kindly twinkle, yet they were not without sharpness on occasion. Modest, timid and even diffident at times, he possessed a quiet charm most effective in small gatherings. He had to do a great deal of public speaking but his clear emphasis was on a thoughtful expression of ideas, not on dramatic presentation. To Woody, "Few, in short, looked like what he was: a college president, shy, earnest, devoted to the causes of education and the church, and anxious to do great good and little harm. He was a scholar yet, all in all, a man of sound judgment. . . . He was a student by preference, a scholar by training, and an administrator only by force of circumstances."

A large measure of Few's success was in articulating a vision and enlisting businessmen, academicians, students, and alumni in the quest. He firmly believed, and won many to share his belief, that historical circumstances developed a special role for Trinity College. When sought by a prestigious midwestern university for its presidency in 1909, Few declined interest, writing, "I believe that circumstances have conspired to give Trinity College a rare opportunity to do a piece of constructive and lasting work in molding the life of a whole people." By 1910 Few was conscious that Trinity had a sense of mission, especially in its native region but also as a model in private higher education in the nation. The college also had a tradition of superior administrative leadership and excellence in faculty, a base of prideful support through the Methodist Church, and, at long last, a degree of financial stability through the benefactions of the Duke family. Few's special role was in understanding the larger framework and in enlisting others, especially James B. Duke, in the fulfillment of a dream.

Another measure of Few's success is that he genuinely enjoyed what he was doing. Late in life he wrote that one of his great privileges had been living intimately with students since he was sixteen. As heavy as were his presidential responsibilities, he frequently was seen about campus. One student guessed that Few probably knew forty percent of the students on West Campus and that he unfailingly greeted you by name with a polite "Good Morning" and tip of the hat. It was not unusual for him to be found umpiring practice baseball games, marking balls and strikes in the dirt with his cane.

At Few's inauguration President Abbott Lawrence Lowell of Harvard University commented that much had been said congratulating Few, but, in truth, the college should be congratulated for selecting Few as president. Lowell's sentiment is more evident half a century after Few's death than it was at the time.

Benefactor Angier Buchanan Duke,
Trinity '05

Writing from the famous Hot Springs resort in Virginia in 1913, Angier B. Duke wired the family's executive secretary to have the chauffeur deliver the limousine to the Princeton Inn for the upcoming Harvard football weekend. On another occasion, poor road conditions posed a problem in getting a car from New York to Durham. Duke drove part way and shipped the car by train for the rest! As the family historian has noted, Angier B. Duke, perhaps more than other family members, enjoyed the particular style of life wealth provided. Not even a hunting accident that cost Duke his right hand slowed him down. He simply had special speed and brake levers fitted in the center of the front seat of his "Torpedo-Phaeton" Rolls-Royce.

Angier Buchanan Duke (1884–1923), son of Benjamin N. Duke, as a Trinity senior in 1905. The Angier B. Duke Scholarships are named in his honor.

While enjoying the benefits of family wealth, Angier B. Duke also acquired the family's interest in education and penchant for philanthropy. Age six when his grandfather, Washington Duke, donated the funds that brought Trinity College to Durham, Angier grew up with his father, Benjamin N. Duke, active on the Trinity Board of Trustees and Building Committee. College personnel were constantly visiting his home and discussing college affairs. Indeed, when his father donated funds for the college's first gymnasium, it was officially named the Angier B. Duke Gymnasium in honor of the then fourteen-year-old boy. Built in 1898, the building now known as the Ark is still standing on East Campus.

After attending Durham public schools, Angier enrolled in Trinity College. He enjoyed college, pledging Alpha Tau Omega fraternity and managing the tennis and baseball teams. He graduated in 1905, cum laude with honors in economics. For a period his sister, Mary Lillian, was a classmate, as she graduated in 1907.

In 1913 Angier was elected an alumni member of the Board of Trustees, and in 1921 and 1922 he served as Vice President and then President of the Alumni Association. Following in the family tradition, he began to make sizable donations to his alma mater with two $10,000 unrestricted gifts. He and his sister also donated $25,000 toward a new gymnasium to be a memorial to alumni killed in World War I. The gymnasium is now known simply as the East Campus Gym.

In April, 1915, Angier B. Duke of New York City married Cordelia Biddle of Philadelphia. At the wedding their sister and brother, Mary Lillian Duke and Anthony J. Drexel Biddle, Jr., announced that their wedding would follow in June. Any information concerning the two families and the marriages became news for the nation's society columns. Eventually Cordelia Biddle, in collaboration with Kyle Crichton, wrote an autobiographical account of her life, focusing to a great extent on her eccentric father. The book entitled *My Philadelphia Father* became the basis for a movie "The Happiest Millionaire" and a play. Unfortunately there are inaccuracies concerning the Duke Family in the popular movie.

Angier B. Duke died tragically and prematurely in a boating accident at age thirty-nine. His loss was felt keenly on campus for he had developed a unique perspective toward Trinity College as a member of the family most involved in its financial support, as a student and alumnus, and as a member of its governing board. In his will he left $250,000 to Trinity College for endowment. But perhaps more significantly, he left the example of yet a third generation of the Duke family immersed in the practice of service and stewardship toward Trinity College. Today his legacy is most evident by the annual awarding of the prestigious Angier B. Duke Scholarships and by the contributions of his sons, the late Angier Biddle Duke and Anthony Drexel "Tony" Duke, to the life of Duke University.

Mary Duke Biddle Continues the Family Tradition of Philanthropy

Over twenty-five descendants of Washington Duke have earned degrees from Trinity College and Duke University. The first in this long line of family graduates were the two children of Benjamin N. and Sarah P. Duke, Angier Buchanan Duke, '05, and Mary Lillian Duke, '07. Their names are recognizable on campus today because of the Angier B. Duke Memorial Scholarships, established in 1925, and the Mary Duke Biddle Music Building, dedicated in 1974. Actually their names were prominent on campus even before they enrolled as students when buildings donated by their grandfather and father were given their names. In 1897 the first dormitory for women, now replaced, was named the Mary Duke Building and in 1899 the first gymnasium, now known as the Ark, was named the Angier B. Duke Gymnasium. In April, 1915 when Angier married Cordelia Biddle of Philadelphia it was announced that his sister, Mary, would marry Cordelia's brother, Anthony J. Drexel Biddle, Jr. the following June.

Today Mary Duke Biddle is recognized as one of the most loyal members of the Duke family as well as one of the most devoted family members to the college turned university by family philanthropy. Born in 1887, she grew to maturity as her grandfather, Washington, generously endowed Trinity College and her father, Benjamin, served on its Board of Trustees and quietly supported the school with annual gifts too numerous to tally. It was her good fortune to first learn about the college as it was overcoming financial troubles and emerging as a first-rate institution. At the turn of the century, Trinity was the pride of Durham, attracting speakers of national renown to the city and providing cultural activities for the industrial tobacco town. Her education in the local schools, study at the Southern Conservatory of Music, and English major at Trinity College helped fashion a lifelong passion for good literature, art and music.

A "Theatre Record and Scrapbook" attests to Mary Duke Biddle's early appreciation of opera and theater, and life in New York City and Irvington-on-Hudson made the cultural amenities she so greatly enjoyed all the more accessible. When the Biddles and Dukes traveled to Newport, Rhode Island for the fashionable summer season, Mary considered it more a duty than fun. Her life centered around her children, first Mary and then Nicholas, and the artists and performers

Mary Lillian Duke (1887–1960), daughter of Benjamin N. Duke, as a Trinity senior in 1907. The Mary Duke Biddle Music building is named for her.

who frequently stayed in her home. Following in her father's footsteps she developed a passion for flowers and gardening as well. Friends noticed eccentricities such as always having cut flowers, even in her car, and her constant playing of an early automatic record player all day and late into the night. Divorce and illness brought sadness to her life, but an indomitable independent spirit and timely medical assistance by Duke's Dr. Frederic M. Hanes saved her life.

Ironically, Mary Duke Biddle followed her daughter, Mary (now Mary D. B. T. Semans) back to Durham where she lived the remainder of her life. Mary's joyous experience as a student at Duke and as a companion to her grandmother, Sarah, enticed her mother back to her hometown. Mary Duke Biddle followed her daughter to Durham where she remained until her death in 1960. Mrs. Biddle constantly invited friends and family to visit and she gloried in the cultural life she found or imported for the university and town. Surprisingly, her only regret with life in North Carolina, she said, was that there was not a sufficient number of women partners for tennis.

The town and university benefited greatly by Mary Duke Biddle's presence. She considered it "a moral family responsibility" to support Lincoln Hospital, the hospital for African Americans founded by her grandfather. Early on, along with her brother, she had made a sizable donation to the Alumni Memorial Gymnasium built in honor of Trinity College students who lost their lives in World War I. Dr. Frederic M. Hanes enlisted her help in planting an iris garden for the university and when that endeavor failed she expanded the project to the formal Sarah P. Duke Gardens in memory of her mother. Another close personal friendship greatly helped the university. First given anonymously, it later was revealed by University Librarian Benjamin E. Powell that the gift in 1948 that enabled the library to double its stack area and create a Rare Book Room was donated by Mary Duke Biddle. Perhaps unique in the university's history, money was left over after the completion of the initial plans. The remaining funds were designated as the first significant endowment for the library. Mary Duke Biddle also purchased the Duke family homestead which had slipped away from the family and gave it to the University along with her father's residence, "Four Acres."

In 1956 the most lasting and far reaching legacy occurred with the creation of the Mary Duke Biddle Foundation. Very conscious of her family's history of philanthropy, Mary Duke Biddle established a trust to further her life-long interests in religious, educational, and charitable activities in the states of New York and North Carolina. By 1995 the foundation had made grants totaling over $20 million. In 1995 trustees under the direction of Dr. James H. Semans made 32 grants for $102,500 in New York, 75 grants for $306,296 in North Carolina, and 80 grants for $491,132 to Duke University. At Duke, grants provided vital support for the Music Department, Art Museum, Institute of the Arts, Film and Video Program and the Cultural Services Program of the Medical Center.

At her funeral service in 1960, Mary Duke Biddle was lauded for "a life founded on the ultimate values of truth, beauty and goodness." Hundreds of thousands of participants in programs and performances supported by the Biddle Foundation can attest to the inspiration of her legacy. Mary Duke Biddle clearly merits recognition as an outstanding member of Duke's founding family and as one of the most influential alumna of the institution.

Southgate Dormitory: Monument to Town-Gown Relations

The momentous announcement of Benefactors' Day in October, 1919, excited both the college community and the townspeople of Durham. Robinson O. Everett, a local attorney and Trinity graduate, announced the formation of the James H. Southgate Memorial Association, the purpose of which was to raise money for a campus building for women students. The building would be the beginning of a coordinate woman's college and that commitment represented a vastly increased emphasis on the education of women at Trinity. It would also mark the culmination of a longtime interest by the popular local businessman and college trustee chairman, James H. Southgate, whose premature death in 1916 had saddened the community.

Southgate, a native of Virginia born in 1859, spent his formative years in nearby Hillsborough before attending the University of North Carolina. At age twenty he put aside his aspirations to be a doctor in order to assist his father who had launched a fire and life insurance business in the rough but promising industrial city of Durham. The growing city benefited greatly from Southgate's business acumen and commitment to religion, culture, and education. Prime local beneficiaries of his lifetime interests were the Methodist Church, the Durham Conservatory of Music, and Trinity College.

Characterized as a man of striking appearance, magnetic personality, balanced judgment and superb oratorical skill, many believed Southgate could win any political office he sought in the state. Putting principle above practicality, however, he left the Democratic Party and joined the National Prohibition Party. He became one of the prohibitionists' most popular speakers, even winning nomination as vice president on their national ticket in 1896.

Southgate served as chairman of the board of trustees of Trinity College for two decades from 1896 to 1916. He played a stalwart role in defend-

James H. Southgate, Chairman of the Board of Trustees from 1896 to 1916, is pictured on the right with President John C. Kilgo.

ing academic freedom during the famous Bassett case in 1902. Southgate's reputation and wise counsel proved invaluable through the years as John C. Kilgo, Trinity's outspoken president, frequently aroused opposition in the church and state.

In 1921, just two years after the announcement of the memorial campaign, Southgate Hall was ready for occupancy. The financial campaign had been a success even though it was conducted during World War I. Citizens of Durham exceeded their goal of $100,000 by $11,000 and B. N. Duke pledged the remaining $100,000 for the ambitious building. Faculty and students even pledged $8,500.

Southgate Dormitory opened in 1921 as "the most complete dormitory for women in the state."

The building, off to the west side of the campus, created great excitement among the women because it afforded almost complete independence from the men. It had sufficient classrooms for the women to take all their first- and second-year courses, except for science laboratory classes, in their own building. It also had a gymnasium, assembly hall, dining room, infirmary and 66 dormitory rooms for 136 students. There were living suites for the dean of women and dining hall matron as well. The *Chronicle* exclaimed that Southgate even had an elevator to transport the women's trunks! This probably was the first elevator on campus.

Extracurricular activities for women expanded or were initiated as a consequence of the welcome additional space. The student government association and YWCA met regularly in the new auditorium and plans were laid for a Woman's Athletic Association, Glee Club, and Drama Club. The local Durham Chapter of the AAUW (American Association of University Women), also met monthly in the new facility.

The enrollment of women at Trinity College gradually increased from 5 in 1892, to 37 in 1902, and 79 in 1912. With the new building in 1921 there were 140 women on campus, the vast majority of whom resided in Southgate Hall. When the Gothic-style West Campus opened in September, 1930, the coordinate college for women became more of a reality with the entire Georgian-style main quadrangle of East Campus becoming the Woman's College of Duke University. Ironically, Southgate then became the only male domain on East. It was turned over to the engineering students who were not to have women colleagues until World War II.

Summing up James H. Southgate's career, a contemporary historian observed that he was a preeminent example of "one of the representative men who will characterize the New South as truly as planters were exponents of the Old South." Southgate Dormitory has remained a fitting tribute to one of Durham's finest citizens and Trinity College's most outstanding servants.

Trinity Committee Formalizes Research Support

One of President William P. Few's persistent themes was that Duke University was built around Trinity College. By that he meant that undergraduate instruction remained central in the university setting and that Trinity's history was crucial to the development of the new university. Earl Porter, the historian of Trinity College, expressed the sentiment another way, stating that in 1924 assets already in possession of Trinity College cushioned the shock of conversion from college to university.

What were some of the assets that undergirded the new university, contributing to its rapid emergence among the nation's elite institutions of higher education? The casual observer credited the successful transition to the philanthropy of the Duke family. Financial support was essential, but acceptance as a research university rested on a more complex foundation. Porter identified the assets as the right personnel for the task and the collective experience or history of the liberal arts college. Certainly Few proved to be the right man as president, but the faculty he largely hired, since he was the college's first dean before he became president, was a crucial contributor as well.

One piece of the foundation for the eventual university emerged in September, 1919, when the first Faculty Committee on Research was appointed. The committee, consisting of James J. Wolfe, Professor of Biology; Thornton S. Graves, Professor of English; and William K. Boyd, Professor of History; had as its charge "the identification of practical measures to foster student and faculty research." Reporting in November, 1919, after interviewing every faculty member, the committee cited two justifications for a greater emphasis on research. Foremost was clearly the positive influence of original investigation on the quality of teach-

William K. Boyd (1879–1938), Professor of History, also served as Director of Libraries.

ing. But significant to the committee as well was the "vital need of creating new research centers in the United States, especially in the South." Noting that centers of intellectual activity were shifting from European countries to the United States, the report emphasized that with very few exceptions these centers were located north of Mason and Dixon's line. Furthermore, the report stated that most specialists who advised the government in the recent World War were from Northern research-centered faculties. These developments were not for lack of native ability in Southerners, because many faculty in these Northern research centers were Southern-born individuals who had located where opportunities and encouragement existed. This Wolfe, Graves, and Boyd knew from personal experience because they were all Southerners who had gone North to Harvard, Chicago, and Columbia, respectively, for their Ph.D. degrees. Each, however, had returned south to Trinity College to begin his professional careers.

The committee made numerous recommendations, all of which were implemented in some form. The first recommendation was that the maximum teaching load be reduced to twelve semester hours per week. Next they sought a sabbatical policy available after six years' service. Traveling expenses to attend both state and national professional meetings were approved. Two Traveling Fellowships of $500 each were recommended for a senior faculty member and either a young faculty member who had not qualified for a sabbatical leave or an exceptional graduate student.

Research grants not to exceed $500 each were requested to provide for a research assistant, or to assist in the publication of research, or to purchase apparatus or books. Demonstrated meritorious research could qualify one for a second or even third award. The selection process was to be administered by a permanent Faculty Research Committee with the awards made by the president of the college at the May faculty meeting.

Recognizing that a research program needed continuing financial support, the committee urged the solicitation of individual and corporate contributions for assistance. A recent faculty appointee in chemistry, Paul M. Gross, began a cooperative effort in tobacco research between his department and the local Liggett and Myers Tobacco Company. This early effort in uniting the academic scientist and the industrial laboratory launched a distinguished career in science administration that ultimately won national and international acclaim for Professor Gross and Duke University.

Building upon the acclaimed series of largely student historical research published by the Trinity College Historical Society, the administration agreed to underwrite a series of research monographs by faculty. The first volume under the imprint of the Trinity College Press almost won instant national prestige for its author and the college. Authenticated accounts reveal that Professor of History Randolph G. Adams' book, *Political Ideas of the American Revolution*, just missed winning the Pulitzer prize for 1922. Its shortcoming was not content but rather its pedestrian appearance due to inattention to design.

Finally, the faculty committee instructed each department head to submit a yearly report to the president citing the number of courses and students taught by each member of the faculty as well as their individual plans and progress for research. The faculty desired an annual record "to inform the President of the burden of teaching and other departmental matters" if indeed research were to become a focus of professional activity as well.

The committee's report on research and its implementation by the administration was but one of several significant initiatives designed to create the best possible college. While university status had been talked about for decades, it was still a dream hardly considered attainable in the immediate future. When the surprise announcement of the Duke Endowment occurred in December, 1924, it was the culmination of quiet, behind-the-scenes discussions which were finalized rather rapidly. Earl Porter, in commenting on the dramatic turn of events, has observed, "The opportunities [for the university] seemed so new and so challenging that it was natural...to forget some realities, especially that there had been a past." That temptation is still present. Reports such as the Trinity College Faculty Committee on Research in 1919 are significant events in the history of Duke University.

Phi Beta Kappa Marks Trinity's Rise in Stature ___

The telegram dated September 17, 1919 reads "Charter granted Trinity without dissenting vote. Congratulations." That telegram, one of the most anxiously awaited notices in the history of the institution, marked Trinity College as a nationally recognized scholarly institution since it granted approval for a chapter of Phi Beta Kappa, the renowned fraternity for scholars. Founded by students from the College of William and Mary in 1776, Phi Beta Kappa's gold membership key is the most prestigious symbol in U. S. higher education. In its first seventy years PBK approved only six charters, but by 1919 it had added eighty-seven chapters on the nation's college campuses. This increasingly fast paced growth worked to Trinity's disadvantage when it first applied for membership.

Trinity had had a local scholastic honorary association since 1890 when John Spencer Bassett, Professor of History, founded "9019." The name recognized the nineteen students with a grade average above ninety and it linked the ideals of learning and service. With the relocation to Durham, financial support of the Duke family, and presidential leadership of John F. Crowell and John C. Kilgo, Trinity College had become a respected regional and increasingly known national institution. Trinity, in fact, had eight faculty members who had earned PBK keys

The initial inductees into Phi Beta Kappa in 1920 included fourteen students and forty alumni.

at such prestigious institutions as Cornell, Yale, Johns Hopkins, William and Mary, the University of Chicago, and Wesleyan and Trinity in Connecticut. These eight members, with Dean William H. Glasson providing leadership, applied for a Phi Beta Kappa chapter for Trinity.

When the Senate of Phi Beta Kappa met in New York City in 1910 it had thirteen applications in hand. No action was taken on six, four were approved, and three, including Trinity, were without explanation "laid over for final consideration" in six years! However, in 1913 Glasson and President Few crafted a campaign urging that the decision on Trinity not be delayed. Despite endorsements from Princeton, Yale, Vanderbilt, Tulane, and the Universities of Missouri, West Virginia and North Carolina, Trinity's application was again postponed.

When the long-awaited year of decision arrived in 1916, the newly constituted Committee on Applications had thirteen pending applications. Again Trinity was carried over "without prejudice." Of this, the third failure, C. S. Northrup of Cornell wrote Glasson, "It had little to do with Trinity." The applications committee simply determined it was "bad policy to continue to expand so rapidly.... Cheer up and have satisfaction that your charter will be worth many times as much" with the new conservative approach.

When consideration arose in 1919, Trinity's file was replete with data about academic requirements, endowment, governance, enrollment, faculty, various scholarly endeavors and the Bassett Affair of 1903, the college's dramatic contribution to the evolving history of academic freedom. Despite the favorable report of an official visiting committee, a question arose. Noting that Professor Bassett had left Trinity for Smith College in 1906, Glasson was queried as to whether Bassett was indeed driven away. The question was easily answered by noting that Bassett had accepted an honorary degree from Trinity in 1916.

The long-awaited telegram of acceptance set off a flurry of activity planning for the chartering ceremony scheduled for February, 1920. Committees were appointed to begin the process of receiving the charter and launching the chapter. The eight current faculty members invited seven administrators to join them as founding members. They determined that alumni members had to have "distinction in letters, science or education" and that eligible students had to have passed all courses on first examination and have grades of 90% or more for six semesters preceding February 1, 1920. Fourteen members of the class of 1920, including six women, were invited to join. Forty alumni, including four women, representing each class since 1879, also were invited to be members. However, a brief campus quarantine due to the influenza epidemic delayed the day of celebration until March 29.

When the day arrived at last, an organizational meeting and a private meeting of induction were held in the afternoon in the Columbia Literary Hall, now the Ernest W. Nelson Music Room, in the East Duke Building. According to the local society reporter "a company of 65 in evening dress sat down to table at an elaborate five course dinner" where after-dinner speeches were given by the Governor of North Carolina, the Chairman of the Trinity Board of Trustees, representatives from the National Council of PBK, alumni and students. Minutes of the planning committee note that a motion to forbid cigars at the banquet was tabled.

Even then the festivities were not over. Public exercises of induction, presided over by President Few, were held in the evening in Craven Memorial Hall with Professor Paul Shorey of the University of Chicago, the nation's foremost Greek scholar, giving an address. A reception at the President's house for all members, visiting delegates, faculty, trustees and officers of the college and their wives concluded the busy day. Obviously Trinity College was pleased to have achieved the "highest recognition of scholarly attainment," election to membership in Phi Beta Kappa. Most significantly, another foundation stone was laid in preparation for the university that was to come.

The original charter of the Trinity College chapter of Phi Beta Kappa.

Why the "Blue Devils"?

In World War I the Chasseurs Alpins or "Blue Devils" were well-known French soldiers. They first gained attention when their unique training and alpine knowledge was counted upon to break the stalemate of trench warfare in their native region of the French Alps. Unfortunately the Vosges Campaign in March, 1915, failed to alter the status quo even though the Blue Devils won accolades for their courage. However, their distinctive blue uniform with flowing cape and jaunty beret captured public imagination. When the United States entered the war, units of the French Blue Devils toured the country helping raise money in the war effort. Irving Berlin captured their spirit in song describing them as "strong and active, most attractive...those Devils, the Blue Devils of France."

As the war was ending in Europe, the Trinity College Board of Trustees lifted its quarter-century ban of football on campus. After playing an intramural class schedule for one year, Trinity began intercollegiate competition in 1920. That first year the traditional nomenclature of the Trinity Eleven, the Blue and White or the Methodists (as opposed to the Baptists of nearby Wake Forest) described the team. In September, 1921, the student newspaper, the Trinity *Chronicle*, launched a campaign for a "catchy name, one of our own possession that would be instantly recognizable nationwide in songs, yells and publicity." At a campus pep rally to stir up enthusiasm it was pointed out that Georgia Tech was gaining recognition as the "Golden Tornadoes" and that rival North Carolina State College had recently adopted the name "Wolf Pack." There were numerous nominations including Catamounts, Grizzlies, Badgers, Dreadnoughts, and Captains which was in honor of the well-liked Coach W. W. "Cap" Card. Believing a choice utilizing the school colors of dark blue and white to be appropriate, the newspaper editors urged a selection from among the nominations of Blue Titans, Blue Eagles, Polar Bears, Blue Devils, Royal Blazes, or Blue Warriors. None of the nominations won strong favor but Blue Devils apparently had enough support to elicit the criticism that it would arouse opposition on the Methodist campus "for obvious reasons," and that it

Recruiting poster for the French Chaussers Alpins or "Blue Devils" of World War I. They derived their name from their dark blue uniform with a distinctive beret and cape.

Silhouette of an early Blue Devil mascot at the traditional pep rally and bonfire before the Duke-Carolina football game.

might prove risky and jeopardize football if a controversial name were used. The football season passed with no official selection of a name.

As the campus leaders from the Class of 1923 made plans for their senior year, they decided to select a name since the desired results by democratic nomination and vote had been inconclusive. The editors of the *Archive* and *Chanticleer* agreed that the newspaper staff should choose a name and "put it over." Thus William H. Lander, as editor-in-chief, and Mike Bradshaw, as managing editor, of the Trinity *Chronicle* began the academic year 1922–23 referring to the athletic teams as the Blue Devils. Their class had been the first post-war freshmen and the student body was full of returning veterans so the name needed no explanation. Acknowledging that it was somewhat unpopular, they nevertheless believed it to be the best name nominated. Neither the college press nor the cheerleaders used the name that first year. In fact, the *Chanticleer* made fun of the selection and process by quoting someone saying "We will use blew devvies even if no one else does." Much to the editor's surprise no opposition materialized, not even from the college administration. The *Chronicle* staff continued its use and through repetition, Blue Devils eventually caught on.

Today the origin of the university mascot is virtually forgotten even though its instant, national recognition has long been established. With the popular Red Devil mascot frequently being challenged throughout the country, the origin of Duke's Blue Devil is one of the most often requested items of information in the University Archives. Questioners are universally surprised to discover its origin is more military and patriotic than religious.

Myths Persist About the Duke Indenture: "The Duke-Princeton Connection"

Perhaps the most frequently asked question of university archivists is verification of the supposed Duke-Princeton connection regarding the beginning of Duke University. One of our most persistent oral traditions is the oft repeated story that James B. Duke offered his significant gift to Princeton University if its trustees would change the name to Duke. They refused. Trinity College in Durham, North Carolina, agreed. Therefore, we are Duke University. Another version that is not as prevalent substitutes Yale for Princeton but Rutgers and Furman are frequently mentioned as well. Sometimes Duke's motivation is addressed by claiming he sought a tax advantage because of the then relatively new federal income tax legislation.

The origins of myths are difficult to pin down but this story may begin with the legal language of the Indenture which established the Duke Endowment on December 11, 1924. Article Four of that legal document reads in part that $6,000,000 will be available to "establish an institution of learning to be known as Duke University." It further provides that if the name of Trinity College be changed to Duke University within three months, then that institution in Durham, North Carolina, would receive the money. At the time the implied quid pro quo received more publicity than it merited in reality. Detractors could not resist claiming that Buck Duke had bought himself a university or bribed a college to memorialize himself.

Presumably Princeton entered the picture because Duke's private estate was nearby in Somerville, New Jersey. Duke had admired Princeton's architecture and as construction proceeded on the new Gothic campus in Durham, maybe similar styles in architecture somehow lent credence to a "Princeton connection." Nevertheless, Article Four of the Indenture clearly stated that the new university had to be in North Carolina, and that the name change was to be a memorial to Wash-

Brass plaque commemorating the creation of the Duke Endowment. Through the family philanthropic organization which continues today, James B. Duke donated, in part, annual support for the new university and money for construction of the two new campuses of the university.

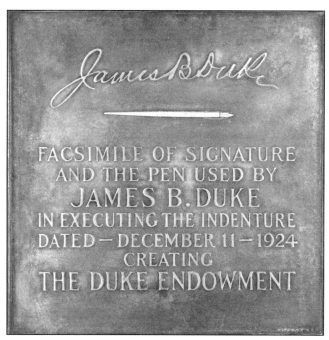

ington Duke, his father, and Benjamin, his brother, and to other family members who so largely contributed to the success of Trinity College since it relocated to Durham. The latter phrase perhaps could be interpreted as an indirect reference to his late sister, Mary, as well as to himself since he had donated a new library building plus $10,000 for books to Trinity College in 1903.

James Buchanan Duke (1856–1925), tobacco entrepreneur, electric power developer and philanthropist.

Fortunately the historical record in the University Archives is not as legalistic or obscure as the Indenture. The idea of building a university around Trinity College and changing the name to Duke is easily attributed to President William P. Few. With a dozen educational institutions named Trinity around the world, Few wanted a clear identity for the new university. James B. Duke reluctantly agreed to the name change.

Motivation, also, is not easily identified. However, the attachment of the Duke family to Trinity College can be dated from Benjamin's election to the Board of Trustees in 1889 and from Washington's donation of $85,000 in 1890 as the principal inducement to attract the college to Durham. Washington later donated $300,000 for endowment and Benjamin quietly began behind-the-scenes contributions to such a variety of Trinity endeavors that the total can never be calculated. Undoubtedly their primary motivation was stewardship as preached in the Methodist Church and Trinity benefited as a Methodist institution. The family's religious stewardship and loyalty to town and state were widely recognized and of long duration. That the brothers acted in concert with and deeply revered their father is a central theme of Robert F. Durden's definitive historical account, *The Dukes of Durham*. While James B. Duke was by far the most well known and wealthiest of the Dukes, his spectacular philanthropy in 1924 was part of a tradition rooted in his family, his church, and his native region. That tradition was more solidly anchored and it clearly predated any income tax legislation or move to New Jersey and passing acquaintance with Princeton University. How other institutions have sometimes been substituted in the story is anybody's guess.

Oral traditions are an integral part of campus life but myths that distort history need to be refuted. Duke University has its own rich history, dating from 1838, that makes it the renowned institution it is today. Have you heard the story of the East Campus wall being ten feet high—three feet above ground and seven beneath? That is an entertaining story but it is not true either!

The Duke Memorial Commissioned to Honor Family

University administrators were so profoundly grateful and admiring of the philanthropy of James B. Duke that they desired a physical memorial to him on campus. However, such a move was not without controversy or even ridicule. A popular assumption, sometimes encouraged by the press, was that the name change from Trinity College to Duke University was sufficient honor and even sought by James B. Duke to gain enduring fame. In truth the name change was at the urging of President William P. Few to distinguish the new institution from a dozen colleges named Trinity around the world. James B. Duke reluctantly agreed and then only if it were understood to be in honor of his father, Washington Duke, and family. Several years after the initial announcement Few despaired of ever having the press accurately represent the reasons for the change.

When the bronze statue of James B. Duke was unveiled in the Chapel court minor controversy flared anew. This time the focus was on the cigar in Duke's hand. Charles Keck, the sculptor, crafted a likeness more realistic than the monu-

The statue of James B. Duke is unveiled as part of the 1935 Commencement weekend.

The sculptor's model for the eight-foot bronze statue of James B. Duke. Charles Keck of New York City crafted the three sarcophagi of the Dukes in the Memorial Chapel as well.

mental, if not almost mythical, representations then often associated with outdoor sculpture. Some students requested the removal of the statue to a less conspicuous place. They feared that the cigar would "attract more attention than the chapel itself" and that the university would be "known as a gift from which the price tag has never been removed." President Few countered saying that careful, fully approved plans always had included a statue of Mr. Duke in the main quadrangle. Moreover Few said, he gladly would do honor to Duke's good deeds in any way, however conspicuous, for the power of his example as a great benefactor and lover of mankind.

Fifty years later the author, Tom Wolfe, again caught the conflicting views as he described the statue as his favorite example of sculpture glorifying the donor of

a building. In a lecture on public art in 1983 Wolfe described Duke's statue as follows: "He is leaning debonairly on his walking stick and has a great round belly and a jolly look on his face and a cigar in his left hand. The statue comes right out and says 'He made a lot of money in tobacco, he gave you this place, he loved smoking, and here he is!'"

The campus memorialization focused on James B. Duke but it, in fact, encompassed the entire family just as the naming of the school included the family. Duke's business colleagues in both tobacco and electric power formed the Duke Memorial Association to raise money for what evolved into three gifts to the university—the family homestead, the Memorial Chapel, and the statue of James B. Duke. Since these gifts were revealed at Commencement in 1935, that June weekend became the long deferred dedication of the new university. Formal ceremonies were never held when the campus opened in 1930.

A major announcement revealed that through the generosity of Mrs. Mary Duke Biddle and the Duke Memorial Association the family homestead had been purchased and donated to the university. The farm and home where Washington Duke's second family had been born and reared had been sold after he moved into the city of Durham. The site also included the modest factories where the family tobacco empire began. It was hoped that such an historic site in conjunction with the spectacular example of family philanthropy illustrated by the new university would be a unique historical example for posterity. The university fulfilled that vision in 1973 by donating the farm and factory to the State of North Carolina for development as an historic site and tobacco museum. Today it is open to the public regularly and listed on the National Register of Historic Places.

Commencement, 1935, also marked the dedication of the Chapel and the completion of the Memorial Chapel in honor of Washington and his two sons, James Buchanan and Benjamin Newton Duke. The Memorial Chapel is an addition to the Chapel of the University though one easily made since it was conceived before construction actually began. The small chapel honors the Dukes as a place for their interment but it also includes a crypt for the burial of family and selected friends of the university. The names of approximately eight thousand donors to the memorial fund are on permanent display in bronze volumes as well.

A unique feature of the Memorial Chapel is the recumbent marble statues of the three Dukes as part of their sarcophagi. Such memorialization is rare in the United States prompting early news accounts to describe the Chapel as the Westminster Abbey of the South. The executive committee of the Memorial Association commissioned Charles Keck for the sarcophagi, as well as for the bronze statue of James B. Duke in front of the Chapel, which was the third project unveiled at Commencement in 1935.

Charles Keck (1875–1951) of New York City was then at the peak of his career. Harry Truman, upon hearing him called America's greatest sculptor, commissioned him for an equestrian statue of President Andrew Jackson for Independence, Missouri. Keck worked in the classical tradition as evidenced by his training with Augustus St. Gaudens, but according to one critic he often exhibited "nervous movement with veristic touches" as well. Two of his more well known works include the larger than life female figure at the entrance to Columbia University and the statue of Father Francis Duffy in Times Square in New York City. Examples in the South of his work include a statue of Booker T. Washington at Tuskegee, Alabama, statues of Stonewall Jackson and Lewis and Clark in Charlottesville, Virginia, and the statue of three United States' presidents from North Carolina in the capital square in Raleigh. Keck's son, Charles, graduated from Duke with B.A. and M.D. degrees in 1949 and 1953, respectively.

In the Memorial Chapel the twenty-ton sarcophagi are of Blanco Puro marble from Carrara, Italy. What began as thirty tons of marble was chipped away and hand finished by rubbing with successively fine polishing stones. Italian workmen at the Hutton Marble Company in Cambridge, Massachusetts created the sarcophagi from clay and plaster models prepared by Keck.

The eight-foot bronze statue of James B. Duke is mounted on an eight-foot-eight-inch pedestal of Cape Anne granite weighing twenty-five tons. The heroic statue with the inscriptions "Industrialist, Philanthropist, Founder of the Duke Endowment," is intended to be an example of a life worthy of inspiration to generations of students. One phrase from the indenture of the Duke Endowment mentions "instruction in history, especially in the lives of the great of the earth." Colleagues of James B. Duke in the business and academic communities were confident that with the Memorial Association's gifts to the university, they were honoring one of the great men of the twentieth century.

The Search for Stone for West Campus _____

In the design and construction of West Campus perhaps one of James B. Duke's greatest satisfactions was the discovery of nearby Hillsborough stone for the Gothic buildings. A participant in that discovery described it as "the kind of a find that delights a construction man's heart," and he perceptively commented that "at heart Mr. Duke was a construction man."

James B. Duke was without question a shrewd businessman as well. After inspecting a half dozen test panels of weathered stone imported from as far as Massachusetts, Duke quietly wondered if suitable stone might not be available nearer at hand. Associates knew such requests were in reality directives for action, but they were fearful of greatly inflated prices if it were known Duke was seeking a vast quantity of building stone. As plans for the development of the university had become known, the price of land surrounding the Trinity College campus had soared. Hence the search for a possible new building stone had to be conducted with utmost secrecy.

Brent Drane, Director of the North Carolina Geological and Economic Survey, reported being quizzed by an official of the Duke Construction Company while on a business trip by train. In a "whispered conversation with extravagant cautions against being seen," Drane was asked where a certain stone native to western North Carolina could be found in quantity. Drane referred the official to Jasper L. Stuckey, the State Geologist. The next day the construction official and Frank C. Brown, a professor of English who also served as university supervisor of planning and construction, visited Stuckey in his Raleigh office with samples of a particular stone in hand. However, before Stuckey could locate that kind of stone a different sample arrived in the mail from Brown with an inquiry as to its identity and availability. Stuckey knew little about the new sample but he remembered seeing some stone similar to it on a residential sidewalk in Chapel Hill. Further inquiry led to Cheshire Webb, a respected businessman in Hillsborough, who matched the sample with pieces from what he called a local "useless old rock pile." Brown visited Webb immediately and had him obtain an option to purchase the seventy-two-acre farm containing the rock for the university.

When James B. Duke visited Durham in March, 1925, to confer with architects, landscape designers, and construction and university officials, he also made a quick trip to Hillsborough to view walls and foundations utilizing the local stone. While quality tests were being conducted by the State Highway Commission and the United States Bureau of Standards, Duke requested that additional viewing panels be erected emphasizing certain desired shades of color. He particularly was elated over the proximity of the farm-quarry to the main railroad line and the fact that it was less than ten miles from the campus construction site. Robert Lee Flowers, Duke Vice President in the Business Division reported that if tests proved the rock suitable, it would mean a savings of two million dollars. The Hillsborough stone cost $3.55 a ton including delivery compared to $15.05 a ton for one of the test panels of Princeton stone. When the building committee selected the stone because of its pleasing color from among unidentified panels everyone was elated.

The Hillsborough stone passed all tests. Called "bluestone" by later quarrymen, the stone had seven primary colors and seventeen different shades of color. Brown wrote the architect, Horace Trumbauer, that the stone had "an older, more attractive antique effect" and a "warmer and softer coloring than the Princeton stone." He particularly liked the fact that the stone could be "laid to give a shadowline underneath the pointing which added tremendously to an artistic look."

Practically speaking, the stone required little effort in quarrying and cutting. Blasting caused cracks so quarrying was done by water pressure and by hand with crowbars. Natural fissures tended to produce stone with four to six faces so even little actual cutting was required. The construction supervisor reported that the stone was "even better than we hoped." The stone is difficult to describe in layman's terms but it is debris somewhat akin to slate from a string of volcanic hills and mountains ranging from Virginia to Georgia. At least 400 million years old, it is volcanic debris changed considerably by heat and pressure and stained by weathering.

In the spring of 1925 what we now call Hillsborough stone was inconspicuous, little known and not even then actively quarried although it had been identified in a state geological survey one hundred years earlier. Quiet research and simple coincidence played a part in its discovery, and its soft, varied color, easy accessibility, low transportation cost and subsequently proven high quality commended it to James B. Duke. In 1937 the English novelist and critic Aldous Huxley wrote of his surprising discovery of an academic "city of gray stone" set in a southern forest in Durham, North Carolina. According to Huxley the Duke West Campus was "the most successful essay in neo-Gothic that I know." For decades Duke University has been the beneficiary of the attractive uniting of a unique local stone and an ancient architectural style.

Sample stone walls were erected on East Campus to aid in the selection of stone for the Gothic campus. The building committee was elated to discover the stone they preferred because of its "seventeen shades of color" was of local origin.

Construction Laborers Unsung Campus Heroes

July 16, 1990 marked the end of an era in the history of the construction of Duke University. On that date Louis Fara, a native of Frugarola, Italy, and the last of the original stone setters who skillfully laid the Indiana limestone trim on West Campus, died. Fara was representative of a group of laborers whose unique background and contribution will be acknowledged as long as eyes gaze upon Duke's majestic Gothic arches.

Documentation of these laborers' contributions is almost nonexistent. Photographs are extremely scarce, since construction took place during the Great Depression and laboring families did not frivolously spend hard-earned money on family snapshots. A few photographs have turned up, usually passport photos of younger men or pictures of much older men working on later commissions. Official university construction photos concentrate on architectural detail instead of the human element. The laborers' background and their sense of accomplishment have to be pieced together from scattered published interviews. Fortunately, their names are familiar, for many remained in Durham to raise their families. Six decades after the completion of West Campus, the city telephone directory still lists the Italian names of Fara, Ribet, Ferettino, Germino, Citrini, and Berini. In addition, Giobbi and Greppi worked the stone as well as the highly respected stone workers Macadie and Brown. They worked along side native African Americans and mountain whites who also had migrated to Durham in search of steady employment during severe economic times.

Each laborer became an accomplished artisan at his assigned level of work. Stonemasons worked the "rubble" bluestone from the nearby Hillsborough quarry. Often thought to be akin to brick layers, stonemasons did not believe the skills were interchangeable. Expert stonemasons had to have a feeling for color and design, as well as the skill to size and shape each stone. These intangible and tangible qualities were vital to the West Campus project where the beauty of the stone was in its seventeen shades of color and where each piece was cut at a ratio of length two times height.

Only the very best men were selected for the more delicate work with "cutstone" or Indiana limestone. They were almost all Italians working for the subcontractor James W. Brown under the supervision of Donald Macadie. Brown and Macadie were natives of Scotland who immigrated to the United States early in the century and located in the south as a result of assigned commissions. The

Italians, too, were most often immigrants who came to Duke as word circulated among friends and relatives that there was stone work in Durham, North Carolina. Many had apprenticed in the Alps of Italy, Switzerland, or France, as had Tony Berini, for a season's pay of "food, lodging, and a suit of clothes, pair of shoes and a bright red cap." In the United States, they were working in New York City or the coal mines of West Virginia before answering the call to Duke. The stone setters set the arches and doorways throughout the campus, capping their employment with the soaring nave of the Chapel. When the campus opened in September, 1930, a select crew remained to finish the Chapel. They were doubly proud because of the special recognition of their expertise and because they were completing such a magnificent structure. It was as if every stone

Jack Ribit, left, and Donald Macadie set the last stone for the Chapel in 1932, marking the completion of the initial construction of the new university.

setter, particularly those with European backgrounds, wanted to work on a Gothic cathedral in their lifetime. As the Duke commission finished many worked on nearby government building projects financed by the New Deal, and some traveled west to build tunnels on the Blue Ridge Parkway.

Very little information is available on the stone carvers who fashioned the decorative sculpture and statuary on campus. Employed by John Donnelly, Inc., of New York, many are believed to have been Irish craftsmen who came to Duke and then returned home upon completion of their work. One *Chronicle* article from November, 1930, cites eight carvers as being at work, but no names are listed in deference to their desire for anonymity. Preferring not to work from models, they drew upon their own experiences and imaginations for the often humorous campus decorative sculpture. One remaining mystery is who selected the subjects for the portals of the Chapel. An anecdotal account has representatives from John Donnelly, Inc., asking Horace Trumbauer, the architect of the university, "Who are the saints of the Methodist Church?" Donnelly and Trumbauer had worked in concert for decades but they had never had a commission quite like the Chapel of the new university. Trumbauer supposedly replied with great amusement to the effect that, "You are on your own. Sculpture does have its problems." It has been assumed that since Sidney Lanier, a popular poet of the New South, is represented that Duke President William P. Few, a South Carolina native and Harvard Ph.D. in English, participated in the selection. The remaining Chapel sculptures are of Thomas Jefferson, statesman; Robert E. Lee, soldier and educator; Girolamo Savonarola, preacher; Martin Luther, reformer; John Wycliffe, translator of the Bible; and Methodist leaders Thomas Coke, Francis Asbury, and George Whitefield, along with John Wesley, the founder of Methodism. The selection of these particular representatives has not been without controversy and amusement.

A distinctive feature of Duke University is having two outstanding examples of collegiate architecture, one American on East Campus and one European on West. As a community we can be thankful for the architects and skilled laborers who constructed our campus. And we, too, should take as much special pride in the campus as they took in building it.

The most dramatic building of the new campus was begun in 1930, first used at commencement in 1932 and dedicated after the installation of the windows in 1935.

"The Laying of the First Cornerstone on the _____ New Campus of Duke University"

On a typically hot summer afternoon on June 5, 1928, the university community gathered for the curiously named ceremony, "The Laying of the First Corner Stone on the New Campus of Duke University." The principal participants were William P. Few, President of the University, George G. Allen, Chairman of the Duke Endowment, Frederick F. Shannon, Pastor of Central Church, Chicago, Edmund D. Soper, Dean of the School of Religion, and Doris Duke, the teenage daughter of the late James B. Duke, benefactor of the university. Promptly at six o'clock a lengthy academic procession wound its way across boardwalks amid construction equipment and mounds of stone to the base of the rising tower of the Union Building. Honored guests included Mrs. James B. (Nanaline Holt Inman) Duke, Mrs. Benjamin N. (Sarah P. Angier) Duke, and Governor Angus W. McLean of North Carolina.

President Few spoke of the meeting of the past and future at the auspicious occasion. In a favorite theme of his, he noted that the new university was being built

The cornerstone ceremony for the Gothic campus was held in 1928 around the corner of the Union Tower.

Miss Doris Duke (1912–1993), the only child of James B. Duke, assisted in laying the cornerstone.

around an old college. "In Trinity College which remains as a part of Duke University," he said, "we have a precious heritage—in its long educational record, its traditions, its ideals, its thousands of graduates." But even amid the clutter of construction, Few noted, in looking about one could easily envisage the new Gothic campus as "fit in every circumstance of beauty and appropriateness to be the home of the soul of Duke University." Anticipating the impact of the impressive architecture, he stated "it would be hard to overestimate the influence that the beautiful surroundings would have upon students and even the character of the institution." In conclusion, Few declared that the university "will be dedicated to truth and disciplined in the hard services of humanity" while following in the example of James B. Duke who "in founding the university cherished the beautiful hope to do some permanent good upon this earth."

At midpoint of the service an impending severe thunderstorm caused Dr. Shannon, the featured speaker, to curtail his address. However, a reporter recorded that "Miss Duke without haste but with the same directness which characterized every act of her father" placed the mortar about the cornerstone concluding the ceremony as rain scattered the crowd.

Careful observation clearly reveals two cornerstones in the main quadrangle today—one on the Union tower and another larger one directly across the quad on the Library tower. When the workmen assembled the following morning after the interrupted ceremony, they discovered that the cornerstone did not fit properly. It was too large for the space allotted in the Union tower. A smaller stone was cut for that space and the original cornerstone containing the sealed box of documents and artifacts was placed in the foundation of the Library tower later. Hence the cornerstone ceremony was held at one place and the actual cornerstone was laid at another. In the interim the stone was altered as well. Photographic inspection reveals that the inscription on the end of the stone—Horace Trumbauer, Architect and Arthur Carl Lee, Engineer and Builder—was added after the original ceremony.

The cornerstone ceremony marked the first participation of Doris Duke in campus functions. She later appeared at official ceremonies celebrating the 100th anniversary of the institution in 1938–1939, at the dedication of the Rare Book Room during the inauguration of President A. Hollis Edens in 1949, at Founders' Day in 1956 honoring the centennial of James B. Duke's birth, and at the retirement symposium for Dean Wilburt C. Davison of the Medical School in 1963.

Architect Julian F. Abele's Life Hidden in Shadows

The original architectural drawings for the proposed campuses of Duke University are true works of art, grand in scale and exquisite in detail. As was common, they are unsigned with the only credit being in the name of the Philadelphia firm of Horace Trumbauer, Architect. The chief designer of the firm and draftsman, Julian F. Abele, in discussing the unique style of the drawings, once proudly proclaimed, "The shadows are all mine." With that statement Abele unknowingly articulated a central fact of his life. As an African American, he lived in the shadows as time and circumstance conspired to conceal his considerable professional talent.

Julian F. Abele (1881–1950) was responsible for both the Georgian- and Gothic-style campuses of Duke University.

At Duke, students discovered Julian Abele in April, 1988. That spring students protesting for Duke's divestment in South Africa built a shanty town in the main quad. A letter writer to the *Chronicle* complained that the ugliness of the crude shelters "violates our rights as students to a beautiful campus." In response, Susan Cook, declared that since the architect of the campus was an African American, he would not have objected to the shanty protest because he was a victim of apartheid in his own country. Indeed, he had not even traveled to view the campus he designed because of his revulsion of segregation then so prevalent in the South. Cook, a graduating senior, had a special interest in the issue. She also revealed that she was the great grandniece of Julian Abele. Her letter caused considerable discussion on campus. The following Spring Duke's Black Graduate and Professional Student Association initiated the annual Julian Abele Awards and Recognition Banquet, unveiling as part of the program, a commissioned portrait of Abele. President Brodie assisted with fundraising and agreed to the hanging of the portrait, the first of a black at Duke, in the foyer of Allen Building.

The student reaction in 1988–89 was in fact a "rediscovery" of Abele. His role had always been known by administrators and careful observers of the university's history. During the design and construction of the institution, Duke administrators constantly visited the office of the architectural firm in Philadelphia. When Professor William Blackburn published a book on the architecture of the university in 1939, he acknowledged that Vice President Robert Lee Flowers arranged for him to interview Abele in his research. One of Julian F. Abele Jr.'s proud possessions is an inscribed presentation copy of Blackburn's book given to his father whose assistance is acknowledged in the preface.

After the death of the founder of the firm, Horace Trumbauer, in 1938, the firm continued for another twenty years but still under the original name. With commissions more difficult to come by during the Great Depression and World War II, it was not a propitious time to change the name of the firm. However, Abele's name began appearing on the architectural drawings in an obvious change of policy. In 1940 when decisions were being made concerning burial in the chapel crypt, A. S. Brower, then assistant to the Comptroller, advised that Abele be consulted because he "prepared the plans and knows the details of the building better than anyone else." Abele's role became more commonly known in 1974 when Alice Phillips published a memoir, *Spire and Spirit,* which tells of her experiences as a long-time hostess in the chapel. Her brief chapter, "Le Noir" tells of her having met Abele's secretary and son on their visits to the chapel.

Horace Trumbauer of Philadelphia founded the architectural firm that designed James B. Duke's New York City residence and the campus of Duke University.

That the contact between Philadelphia and Durham was one way for Julian Abele is hard to comprehend today but more understandable when one delves into the circumstances. Trumbauer was heard to say "I hire my brains." In truth Abele was too valuable to have away from the firm. Although acknowledged as a premier builder of gilded age palaces, often in the grand French style, for the wealthy in Philadelphia, Newport and New York City, Horace Trumbauer incredibly had no formal education having dropped out of school at age sixteen. He learned the profession as an apprentice draftsman and through voracious reading. When he began his own firm in 1890, he hired exceptionally qualified personnel, held them to very high standards, and paid them handsomely if they could work together. Extremely self conscious about his lack of education, he deliberately sought anonymity preferring to work one-on-one with his wealthy clients relying on their recommendations for commissions.

Trumbauer instantly recognized the talent of Julian Abele when he observed some of Abele's student award winning drawings. Upon Abele's graduation in 1902 as the first black student in architecture at the University of Pennsylvania, Trumbauer financed further study for him at the Ecole Des Beaux Arts in Paris. Abele joined Trumbauer's firm in 1906, advancing to chief designer in 1909.

Because of his talent and aloofness, Trumbauer gained accolades in New York City before he did in his hometown. His colleagues in Philadelphia did not elect him to membership in their chapter of the American Institute of Architects (AIA) until 1931, an affront that reportedly greatly disturbed him. Added to this mix was the fact that he employed, advanced and befriended one of the very few African American architects in the country. Trumbauer and Abele each faced discrimination and because of that Trumbauer empathized with the racial discrimination confronting Abele. Consequently they forged a close relationship based on respect for talent and friendship, but each also trapped the other in a peculiar set of circumstances. Trumbauer excelled as the front man dealing with major clients but he avoided publicity and public appearances. Abele was the African American chief designer essential to the internal operation of the firm, a position too confining for his deserved reputation. Abele, himself, was not elected to membership in the Philadelphia AIA until 1941.

Along with many houses for the Elkins and Widener families as well as for the Kimballs, Belmonts, Drexels, and Stotesburys, the Trumbauer firm designed the residence of James B. Duke in New York City and a proposed residence in Somerville, N.J. Presumably that is why the firm received the commission to design the new university bearing the Duke name. Unfortunately the partners who carried on after Abele's death in 1950 destroyed the firm's records. Sadly, a lack of records further contributes to the shadow which engulfs the life of Julian F. Abele and obscures the role of the architectural firm of Horace Trumbauer.

[This article is based on personal interviews and *The Twilight of Splendor: Chronicles of the Age of American Palaces* (1975) by James T. Maher.]

Building a University:
The Bottom Line _____

The final report of the Duke University Building Committee of the Duke Endowment, dated June 28, 1932, is fascinating for its account of the cost of the construction and equipping of both East and West Campus. The committee had $21,254,833.69 total funds at its disposal. It expended $4,782,710.57 for the new Georgian style portion of the Woman's College or East Campus and $16,373,421.84 for the new Gothic West Campus. Included in the figures are the purchase of 5,080 acres of land. Not included is the expenditure of $1,124,195.75 of university financing for a gymnasium, stadium, athletic practice fields, and twelve residences. The Duke Construction Company under the general supervision of A. C. Lee, Chief Engineer, constructed a Medical School and Hospital of 4,429,000 cubic feet, an East Campus of 6,350,000 cubic feet and a West Campus of 12,508,000 cubic feet. There is little wonder that a headline in the local newspaper once trumpeted "Largest Building Permit in the History of the South Issued Here Today."

The original Trinity Durham campus was rebuilt in the Georgian style between 1925 and 1927. It served as the Woman's College from 1930 until it was merged with Trinity College in 1972.

As interesting as is the aggregate report of the building committee, an addendum appearing in November, 1932, offers a detailed look at the construction of the focal point of the campus, the chapel. Begun last just as West Campus was being occupied for the academic year 1930–31, the chapel was being readied for its first use at Commencement, 1932 when the final accounting was being made. Essentially complete except for the installation of the stained glass windows, the cost of the most expensive building on campus was listed at $2,285,742.54. On an impressive new campus, superlatives abounded in describing the chapel. With foundation walls 20-feet thick and an imposing tower of 210 feet uniquely placed forward over the narthex, the chapel, by design, dominated the campus. It contained more of the native Hillsborough stone than the hospital and half as much Indiana limestone as in all of the additional Gothic buildings.

Fifty-one percent of the chapel's total cost was for the stone: 18 percent for the rubble bluestone and 33 percent for the cut limestone. With no structural steel as in the rest of the campus, the architectural design supports the soaring building just as in European cathedrals. The only steel, less than one half of one percent of the total cost, supports the roof above the vaulted ceiling, a concession to fire protection in case lightning strikes Mr. Duke's "towering church." Nine percent of the building cost was for the stained glass windows and 8.5 percent was for the hand carved woodwork and paneling. The Aeolian organ ($65,300) and carillon ($54,500) accounted for 5 percent of the total cost.

A new Gothic-style campus was built for the expanded university between 1927 and 1930.

Committee reports tally cubic feet and dollars and cents but a distinguished visitor, the English novelist Aldous Huxley, captured the spirit of the new campus. Writing in 1937 he described traveling through "a pleasant but unexciting land" when "all of a sudden, astonishingly a whole city of gray Gothic stone emerged from the warm pine forest." He was thrilled by the "leaping tower" of the huge cathedral and the "spreading succession of quadrangles." He called the campus "genuinely beautiful, the most successful essay in neo-Gothic that I know."

Indiana limestone trim for the Gothic campus.

The Fifty-Bell Carillon:
A Unique Gift

In April, 1930, President William P. Few opened a letter from George G. Allen and William R. Perkins, Chairman and Vice-Chairman of The Duke Endowment, which began, "We desire to present to the University a carillon for installation in the tower of the church which is now under construction...." Despite imminent departure from campus, Few penned a hasty but heartfelt reply saying, "It is a beautiful gift you have made. The Chapel bells will in a sense be the voice of the University, and it is most appropriate that this voice should come through the two men now living who were most intimately associated with Mr. James B. Duke."

The surprise gift was unique but most fitting for the 210-foot Chapel tower beginning to rise from its foundations. Carillons had a long history dating from the 16th century in Belgium and Holland. They had evolved from chimes and were mostly associated with municipal timepieces in a centrally located clock tower. However, the instrument passed into decline in the 18th century, in part due to the death of bellfounders who always had guarded their secrets for casting finely tuned bells. Also the advent of private indoor clocks and watches and the

From the left, President W. P. Few, Vice Presidents W. H. Wannamaker and R. L. Flowers, and a representative from the London bell foundry inspect three bells for the carillon as they arrive on campus.

popularity of the concert hall for musical performance relegated the surviving carillons to the status of museum pieces subject to deterioration and changing fashion. It was not until the 20th century that a revival of interest in carillons occurred and not until 1922 that the first one was installed in the United States. It is not known why Allen and Perkins selected a carillon as a gift for the University but one can speculate that they got the idea from the installation of a carillon at Park Avenue Baptist Church in New York City in 1925. Residing in New York, they undoubtedly saw the extensive publicity concerning the installation of that large fifty-three bell carillon.

The Duke carillon was cast by the Taylor Bell Foundry of Loughborough, England, heirs to a succession of foundrys dating to 1360. Most significantly the firm, along with only one other, assumed the lead in perfecting the casting and tuning of a perfect set of bells, thus initiating the 20th-century renaissance in carillons. The size of the largest bell and the range of scale distinguish the character and importance of a carillon more than its total number of bells. The Duke carillon has 50 bells ranging over four chromatic octaves varying in weight from 10 to 11,200 pounds and in size from 8 inches to 6 feet, 9 inches in diameter. While not the largest, the combination of size, number, and tonal quality make the Duke carillon one of the more outstanding examples of that ancient instrument.

Modern carillons tend to be electronically played such as those nearby at North Carolina State University and the University of North Carolina at Chapel Hill, but hand playing is vastly superior as it is the only way to develop any gradation of volume or tone. Playing is hard work. One pounds the keys with the downward stroke of a slightly balled fist. In reality the keys are more like levers which pull a mechanism that pulls the clapper against a stationary bell. Force sufficient to move clappers sometimes weighing over one hundred pounds is required to strike the larger bells.

Duke has had only two individuals designated as the University Carillonneur. The first from 1932 until 1956 was Anton Brees, a native of Belgium, who divided his time between the Bok Singing Tower at Lake Wales, Florida, and Duke. His inaugural Duke recital on commencement weekend, 1932, attracted 10,000 people. The current carillonneur, J. Samuel Hammond, was designated University Carillonneur by President Brodie in 1986. Hammond, trained in piano and organ, began playing the carillon in 1965 while an undergraduate student in history. A member of the Guild of Carillonneurs of North America, he is also Rare Book Librarian in Perkins Library.

Acknowledging that the carillon is a very public instrument, Hammond tries to respond to public occasions in his daily concerts. He begins by ringing the five o'clock hour with the largest bell. Then by careful listening one can usually identify the current religious, holiday or patriotic occasion by the selections being played. Sometimes "Raindrops Keep Falling On My Head" is appropriate for the day. If one is curious about a selection for a given day, Hammond's personal log is on file in the University Archives. One welcome tradition is the rendition of the alma mater, "Dear Old Duke," every Friday afternoon.

To many in the University community, the carillon is a most pleasant "voice," always enjoyed on special occasions, but especially welcome Sunday morning and at the end of each workday.

Divinity School Founders Believed in High Standards

In September, 1926, the new university's first professional school, then called the School of Religion and now known as the Divinity School, opened its doors. It was an inauspicious time to be launching a professional school in the South dedicated to the academic training of clergy. National attention had been riveted on the fundamentalist wing of Southern Christianity during the recent Scopes trial over the teaching of evolution in the public schools of Tennessee. A survey of Methodist clergy in the South revealed that 53 percent had a high school education or less, 11 percent had a college education, and only 4 percent had training both in college and a theological seminary. It was difficult to discern whether potential for a School of Religion was so great that success would soon follow or the obstacles so large, it would take a long time to succeed.

That Duke's first new professional school was a School of Religion was not surprising. The institution had a religious affiliation since 1838 when Methodists and Quakers joined forces to form Union Institute to permanently educate their children. More formal ties emerged with the Methodist Church and in 1859 the school became Trinity College with the motto, Eruditio et Religio. In 1890 the future of the college became forever linked to the wealthy Duke family when church ties led to Trinity becoming the primary focus of the family's philanthropy. In 1924 at James B. Duke's behest, the indenture creating Duke University read in part, "I advise that courses be arranged, first, with special reference to the training of preachers, teachers, lawyers and physicians, because.... by precept and example they can do most to uplift mankind...." There was no more willing advocate than President William P. Few who had long sought to increase limited curriculum offerings in the preparation of preachers. The Duke gift presented the opportunity to move beyond undergraduate instruction provided in part through support from the local conferences of the Methodist Church.

From the beginning it was clear that the School of Religion was to be ecumenical, staffed by first-class academically trained faculty, and subject to high standards. As the college became a university, Few's first selection as Dean was Edmund D. Soper, a New York Methodist then teaching at Northwestern University. His degrees were from Dickinson College and Drew Theological Seminary. Also added to the faculty were Elbert Russell, a Quaker, who came

The Divinity School symbol, carved in stone over the entrance, shows the Church as a ship in which the faithful find salvation from the storms of life.

Edmund D. Soper (1876–1961) was appointed Dean of the first professional school of the university, the School of Religion, in 1926.

from a position at Swathmore College and had degrees from Earlham College and the University of Chicago, and Bennett Harvie Branscomb, a Methodist with undergraduate training at Birmingham-Southern College and two degrees from Oxford University. Already on the Duke faculty were James Cannon III in Religion, who was educated at Trinity and Princeton, and Paul Neff Garber, a former member of the Church of the Brethren who had become a Methodist. Garber transferred from the history department where he was teaching with a Ph.D. degree in history from the University of Pennsylvania. Russell, Garber and Cannon were to become Deans of the Divinity School, and Branscomb was to be Director of the Libraries at Duke and a distinguished Chancellor of Vanderbilt University.

Candidates for admission to the School of Religion had to be graduates with certified transcripts from colleges of recognized standing. Women were admitted on the same conditions as men and either a local pastor, church official, or college professor had to attest to the applicant's Christian character and purpose. Graduation was dependent upon satisfactory completion of ninety semester hours of work, usually taken in three years, plus the approval of a written thesis.

With a minimum of publicity, twenty-three students, twenty men and three women, enrolled the first year. Twenty students were graduates of Trinity and Duke with degrees earned between 1906 and 1926. All but two were from North Carolina. Within five years enrollment reached one hundred fifty, with students from eighteen states and Korea and Japan. While fifty-three percent were from North Carolina, every southern state as well as eight additional states were represented. Students from over forty undergraduate colleges enrolled with Duke continuing to provide the most by a large margin.

The School of Religion achieved recognition rapidly for offering above average training for all types of Christian service. While focusing clearly on the role of the minister in a local church, the school also sought to prepare missionaries, teachers, directors of religious education and social workers. Proud of its Methodist heritage and ties, the school, nevertheless, was conducted on ecumenical and not narrow denominational lines. But above all, it was launched on the strong conviction that the education offered should be based on standards of the highest level.

Dean William H. Glasson Directs Growth in Graduate Studies

The signing of the Duke Indenture in 1924 marked a dramatic departure for Trinity College, but in some cases it simply accelerated commitments already made. In graduate education, the college had awarded masters degrees for decades but the nineteenth-century M.A. was almost honorary in comparison to the twentieth-century research based degree. The commitment to modern graduate education was formalized in 1916 with the appointment of the first permanent faculty committee on graduate instruction. Unfortunately, World War I erupted as the committee's recommendations were being implemented. Demand, however, was accelerated with the influx of post-war students. Thirty-five non-law graduate students in 1923 represented a three-fold increase over pre-war enrollment.

A 1923 report of the committee on graduate instruction established a master of education degree in addition to the master of arts degree, required a written thesis for each with a defense before a faculty committee, and more clearly differentiated between undergraduate and graduate level instruction. The move toward graduate instruction with high standards was well underway when Trinity College became Duke University.

President William P. Few formally recognized the graduate program as a constituent part of the new university in 1926 with the appointment of William H. Glasson as Dean of the new Graduate School of Arts and Sciences. Glasson, trained at Cornell and Columbia, had been at Trinity as Professor of Political

William H. Glasson (1874–1946), Professor of Political Economy and Social Sciences.

Economy and Social Sciences since 1902. Few and Glasson believed that, more than anything else, the Graduate School would determine the standing of the university in the educational world.

The two administrators were not disappointed by the spectacular growth in graduate enrollment. In the 1927–28 academic year, the Graduate School enrolled 128 students representing 48 undergraduate institutions and 20 states plus China. Glasson proudly proclaimed that "the Graduate School has a spirit and background far different from a merely local institution." He felt very strongly that the varied background of the students and the research emphasis of the graduate school contributed vitally to the academic atmosphere of the new university. Perhaps more than anyone except Few, Glasson understood the importance of the interrelation of the component parts of the new institution. He had almost single-handedly achieved the awarding of a Phi Beta Kappa chapter to Trinity College in 1919. He also constantly emphasized that the professional schools of the university would be vitalized and enriched by a research centered graduate school. To that end Glasson won approval for students in the medical school and departments of biology, chemistry and psychology to take each other's advanced courses.

The Graduate School experienced growth despite the deepening economic depression. In the spring of 1931, there were over 600 applicants for 27 fellowships and 21 scholarships and assistantships. Working closely with the Director of the Summer Session, Glasson scheduled graduate offerings in the summer term equal in quality to the winter academic courses. Such an arrangement employed faculty year around, enhanced choices by offering courses like travel abroad or field experience through botanical stations in the mountains or on the coast, and enabled students to earn credits faster, thus incurring less financial debt. In the summer of 1930, 447 of the 1,212 students enrolled, or 37 percent, were degree candidates in the Graduate School of Arts and Sciences.

Few and Glasson were equally proud of the quality of additions to the faculty and of faculty research and publications. The reputation of the university grew immeasurably with faculty additions like William McDougall in psychology, Charles Ellwood in sociology, Jay Hubbell in English and Shelton Smith in religion. Research in Japan by zoologist A. S. Pearse, and in Russia and Spain respectively by economists Calvin Hoover and Earl Hamilton resulted in publications that brought prestige to the new graduate school and university.

The institution awarded its first doctor of philosophy degrees in 1928 to Frederick Holl and Dean Rumbold in zoology. In 1929 Rose May Davis became the first woman to earn a doctorate when she was awarded the Ph.D. degree in chemistry. In the late 1990s, Duke began awarding more graduate and professional than undergraduate degrees.

Dean Alice Mary Baldwin
Fought for Equality

In 1964 the most prominent building on East Campus was dedicated as the Baldwin Auditorium in honor of Dean Alice Mary Baldwin, one of the most significant administrators in the history of the university. Initially coming to Trinity College in 1923 as Dean of Women and the first woman to have full faculty status, she became Dean of the new undergraduate college for women in 1926, a position she held until her retirement in 1947. In 1959 she wrote a memoir "to be opened in twenty years" outlining her aims, accomplishments and frustrations as the university's first major female administrator. Although longing for equal recognition with the men on campus for herself as well as for the female faculty and students, she realized that time and circumstance probably precluded such recognition for her. Nevertheless, her reminiscences clearly articulate a desire for total equality and document her diligent work toward that end for all women in the university community. The fact that she was a trained historian writing for posterity adds immeasurably to the value of the document.

Alice Mary Baldwin (1879–1960) became Dean of the Woman's College in 1926.

The task before her was enormous. The governing male administrators were aware of the need for vital decisions on the Woman's College concerning admissions, housing, curriculum, discipline, and the logistics of scheduling classes and transportation. They hardly gave a thought to Dean Baldwin's personal primary concern of "desiring recognition as a fellow administrator, not simply as a woman to be treated with Southern courtesy." She was, in fact, at times not treated with courtesy, but through her long career she did win considerable respect. She retired proud of her accomplishments in the Woman's College and of its role in the developing university. Unfortunately, the equality for which she worked so hard would emerge slowly, but it has developed in large measure because of the foundation she laid.

The decision for a co-ordinate college for women had been made prior to Baldwin's arrival. When queried by President Few as to her philosophy, she replied she preferred co-education but that her "job was to make the Duke co-ordinate college the best possible of its kind." To that end, she carefully crafted a student experience that encouraged initiative and responsibility through self-government. The Woman's College governed itself through its own student government association and judicial board with participation centered in dorm or House Councils and with an influential House President. When the students discovered they could indeed make their own rules, they liberalized dating and lights out regulations while holding to rules against smoking and drinking. Taking their role very seriously, student leaders established training classes in parliamentary procedure, a civil service exam board for officers, and a point system based on positions of responsibility in order to ensure that student leadership was not the exclusive right of a select few.

Dean Baldwin pushed leadership training a step further by creating local chapters and encouraging participation in state and national women's organizations such as the League of Women Voters and the American Association of University Women. She practiced what she preached by becoming a member of perhaps two surprising organizations, the Durham Chamber of Commerce and the Daughters of the American Revolution. Though she disagreed with certain positions of these national organizations, she joined the local chapters because she believed her participation would win community support for women and the Woman's College. Dean Baldwin's foremost example of service came with her acceptance of President Franklin D. Roosevelt's invitation to be one of eight advisors to the United States Navy in establishing the WAVES, the Navy's Women's Reserve, during World War II. Learning from their own experiences and her example, students successfully launched such varied organizations as a Forum Committee to invite speakers to East Campus, *Distaff*, a monthly magazine edited entirely by women, the Nereidians, a synchronized swimming club, and numerous honorary and leadership societies such as Ivy, Sandals and White Duchy.

In the crucial realm of participating in university governance, Baldwin had mixed results. She pushed hard for the employment of female faculty with the same high credentials as men. By 1930, there were ten female faculty members in rank from instructor to full professor. Baldwin, herself, taught the first advanced level course offered by a woman in the university. She clearly established the equality of the Woman's College with other schools by developing its own set of administrative officers, its own advising and records system, and its own admissions program. However, she had to be constantly on alert. Her advice was solicited in designing furniture for the women's dorms, but her request to meet with Horace Trumbauer, the architect, to discuss more substantive issues was never granted. When a faculty committee recommended abolishing the twenty minute interval between classes, she successfully fought for its continuance explaining how such a change would limit choice and access to certain classes and professors for the women who resided on East Campus.

Perhaps "passing the buck," President Few gave Baldwin permission to abolish sororities if she thought it best. After careful consideration, she retained those in existence and even encouraged their growth because if men had fraternities she certainly did not want to discriminate against women. But sororities were to exist only if they continued without distinctive residential status. She wanted primary loyalty to be to one's dorm and the Woman's College. Furthermore, new sororities including national ones had to pass a period of probation before acceptance.

Dean Baldwin was so successful in launching the Woman's College that tension sometimes arose with other schools. The selective admissions policy and consequent high academic performance of the women kept pressure on Trinity College, the undergraduate college for men, to strive for excellence.

When Alice Baldwin arrived on campus approximately 200 women lived in Southgate dorm. At her retirement in 1947 the Woman's College occupied all of East Campus and its undergraduate enrollment totaled 1,128. A true measure of her success was that far more women sought admission to the Woman's College than could be accepted. Dean Baldwin's ninety page memoir is one of the most significant documents in the Duke University Archives. It clearly states her philosophy and illustrates her considerable achievements. Even though the Woman's College has been merged with Trinity College since 1972, its history is very much a vital part of the excellence of Duke University. Baldwin Auditorium is apt recognition for one of Duke's most important figures.

The focal point of East Campus was named Baldwin Auditorium in 1964 in honor of one of Duke's most significant administrators, Dean Alice Mary Baldwin of the Woman's College.

A New Football Stadium and the Opening of West Campus

Duke University was created in December, 1924 long before the woods were cleared for a new campus over a mile to the west of the original Durham site. An answer to the question, what facility was used first on the new West Campus, might well provide a surprising answer. The most publicized events are the opening of the hospital on July 1 and the beginning of the academic school year in September, 1930. However, the first use of any West Campus facility occurred nine months earlier on October 5, 1929 when the Blue Devils played the Pittsburgh Panthers in the new football stadium! Students and fans had to be bussed from the recently redesigned East Campus around the construction of the Gothic campus to the completed stadium for its dedicatory game. That such an impressive facility was available is truly remarkable considering Trinity College had reinstated football only in 1920 after a self imposed ban of twenty-four years. Despite a fitful start with seven different coaches in nine years the administration and athletic council were carefully planning for the future.

In 1929 football moved from the limited playing area along Broad Street on East Campus to a state-of-the-art 35,000-seat stadium on West Campus.

Athletics clearly were to be part of the new university. Even though the physical facilities were on the periphery of the campus, the playing fields and gymnasium were to be "thoroughly in keeping with the beauty and dignity of the new Gothic campus." The gymnasium, soon named after the popular coach W. W. "Cap" Card, was of the same design, stone and trim as were the nearby Gothic buildings. The all purpose gym contained facilities for physical education, a swimming pool, and a basketball court. A distinctive stadium with seating for 35,000 and facilities for football and track and field was planned for an adjacent natural ravine. Once design was determined the impressive stadium was constructed in a remarkably brief time.

Stadium construction was outside the original monetary commitment to build the university. For financing, the athletic council issued certificates of indebtedness at 6% interest. Alumni and friends were urged to buy the bonds with one appeal being for "1,000 individuals to invest $100 in Duke's athletic future." Investors were told they could provide an outdoor stadium unique in the south with entrance from the top like those at the Universities of Pittsburgh, Washington and California. Unobstructed vision was guaranteed by curved seating with the bottom row elevated six feet and the top row forty feet above the playing field. The cinder track was a quarter-mile in length with two 220-yard straightaways.

The financial campaign was successful with alumni anxious to view the football teams that such a capacity stadium would attract with the customary sharing of the "gate" for visiting teams. Payment of all obligations was assured, despite the deepening economic depression, when one of the best known coaches in the country, Wallace Wade of the University of Alabama, expressed interest in Duke's athletic program. When asked to recommend a coach, Wade surprised the administration with his own interest in the position. He later confided that the leadership of the university, the opportunity to return to a private university and the offer to direct the total athletic program greatly appealed to him. Two home games with the powerful Pittsburgh program illustrate Wade's accomplishment. Before his arrival the inaugural game was an embarrassing 57 to 7 loss in front of a sparse crowd. In 1938 Wade's eighth team defeated Pittsburgh 7 to 0 in a snowstorm to preserve an undefeated, untied and unscored upon season and secure Duke's first Rose Bowl invitation. The second Rose Bowl acceptance with Duke hosting the game because of the surprise attack at Pearl Harbor in 1941 is an often told story. That is the only time in the history of the Rose Bowl that the game has been played away from California. Success gave rise to success. Income from the 1939 Rose Bowl appearance provided impetus to build a new gymnasium. Again administrators clearly were planning for the future when the new basketball arena proved to be the largest south of Philadelphia.

Track and field events in the stadium have brought thrills and international renown to the university as well. In 1956, Dave Sime, perhaps the most electrifying of Duke athletes, was billed as the "World's Fastest Human." As a sophomore, Sime, an unheralded baseball player, burst on the track scene setting world records in a winter indoor meet in Washington, D. C. When he appeared outdoors at Duke in the spring, large crowds were not disappointed. In a single meet Sime set the world record in the 220-meter low hurdles, tied the world record in the 220-yard dash, and missed the world record in the 100-yard dash by just ⅒ of a second. Continuing to compete while in medical school, Sime went on to hold seven world records and earn Olympic medals despite injury and a rigorous academic schedule.

Ever conscious of providing the best performing surface possible, the cinder track of Sime's day has been replaced and resurfaced numerous times. The football field even has been moved to permit the construction of an eight-lane Olympic size 400-meter oval track. With state-of-the-art facilities and the expertise of track coach and respected administrator Al Buehler, Duke has hosted over half a dozen international track meets including the Pan African-USA Games and USA-USSR dual meets. In 1974 track and field reigned in Durham as 65,000 spectators attended the two-day Soviet-American meet. Lyudmila Bragina broke her own world record in the 3,000-meter run acknowledging that the tremendous ovation of the crowd spurred her on. Additional major track events have been hosting the NCAA Division I Collegiate Championships in 1990 and a warm-up meet for the 1996 Olympics in Atlanta.

Once during his tenure, President Few gratefully thanked the athletic department for being of "invaluable assistance in making and keeping Duke University a busy, happy, safe, and helpful place for youth." He might well have added for alumni and friends too. Duke Stadium, officially known as Wallace Wade Stadium since 1967, has played an appropriate role in campus life since 1929.

The Opening of a New Gothic Campus

The beginning of the academic year 1930–31 was probably the most exciting in the history of the institution. Duke University came into being in December, 1924, and for five long years, as the old campus was largely rebuilt and as professional schools were added, everyone shared the cramped quarters of what is now East Campus. Then in September, 1930, a large impressive new Gothic campus was available for use. A twenty-two million-dollar plant with fifty-one new buildings (20 for the co-ordinate college for women on East and 31 on West) became the home of Duke University. When school opened the campus news service was issuing daily releases to 235 newspapers nationwide because of the intense interest in the new university. In campus ceremonies President William P. Few conveyed the excitement in appealing to each student "to catch the thrill of living in the midst of an institution is in the building."

That fall semester of 1930 every issue of the weekly *Chronicle* seemed to announce major changes in some aspect of campus life. The most apparent change was an increase in enrollment, especially in the dramatic addition of women. Official undergraduate enrollment totaled 1,785 including 1,314 men and 471 women, an increase of 91% enrollment of women in one year. In addition, the

The Gothic West Campus opened for residency and classes in September, 1930.

Graduate School had 138 men and 62 women in its largest enrollment ever, the Law School had 77 men and 2 women, and the Medical School opened with 66 men and 4 women. In five years the School of Religion had increased its enrollment from 18 to 131. The student body had representation from twenty-eight states and six foreign countries.

"Cap" Card, the popular director of physical education recorded annual statistics on all freshmen men. His eagerly awaited compilation for the entering Class of 1934 reported an average height of 5'7" with the tallest being 6'2" and the shortest an even 5'. The average weight was 137 pounds with the heaviest at 208.

The physical arrangement of the campus placed the men and professional schools on West, the women in the Woman's College on East, and the engineers in Southgate near their instructional campus in Bivins, Branson, and Asbury buildings. Despite an arrangement that wags characterized as a co-ed school with a mile-and-a-quarter hyphen, President Few emphatically stated that men and women enjoyed equal advantages with any course offered only on one campus being open to all. The hospital in the Medical Center reported a capacity of 408 beds with 99 patients registered on October 1. They were served by 61 physicians and 43 faculty.

The social scene livened up considerably with officially sanctioned dances on campus for the first time. "Jelly" Leftwich directed the University Club Orchestra for most of the dances in the new Union Ballroom, now the faculty commons. The dances were dutifully chaperoned by university officials. Quadrangle Pictures in the recently named Page Auditorium boasted of its "$30,000 projection set which had no equal nearer than Birmingham, Alabama." When the Board of Trustees officially named all the buildings, Page had the unique distinction of being named after two individuals—Walter Hines Page, alumnus and former Ambassador to the Court of St. James, and his nephew Allison Page, the first Trinity student to give his life in World War I. Concern for safety dictated the first ever required registration of automobiles with 72 student cars accounted for by mid-semester. A continuing debate with cycles of arrests for traffic violations swirled around whether the campus drive was private university property or under the jurisdiction of city police.

The year brought sweeping changes in the grading system with the introduction of letter grades—A for exceptional; B, superior; C, medium; D, inferior; and F, failure. Averages were computed by assigning 3 quality points per semester hour for an A, 2 for a B, 1 for a C, 0 for a D, and –1 for an F. In a plea for equality and perhaps feeling academic pressure, co-ed editorials noted that the library on West remained open an hour longer until 10:30 p.m. Also with the transfer of so many books to West, one had "a barren, futile feeling" about empty shelves in the Woman's College library. The women also requested more buses to transport them to classes on West. The co-eds believed that the nickel fare should guarantee arrival on time for class and without having to stand on one foot in an overcrowded bus.

In October, the *Chronicle* reported on the cornerstone ceremony for the Chapel. The foundation was just beginning to rise and the Chapel's projected size was hard to comprehend. A foreman reported that it would contain half the Indiana limestone as in all other buildings, and more native stone than the new hospital. Noting that the Chapel would not be completed for two years, the *Chronicle* editorialized that the goal of James B. Duke truly had not been reached either. "Despite the physical beauty of the new campuses and nearly a century of tradition, the success of Duke University remained to be measured. That success would be determined by the ability of the university to turn out men and women better fitted for life than when they entered. Whether Duke is to become an appreciable force in American civilization or merely a majestic skeleton, noted the *Chronicle*, depends on the conduct, attitude, effort, and accomplishment of the individuals it harbors."

West Campus in 1931 with the chapel under construction on the right.

Academic Freedom in the 1930s: Controversy Over a Speech by Norman Thomas _____

In June 1901 — as is often the fashion with a "new era" — President John C. Kilgo included a statement of the spirit and aims of Trinity College in his first report of the new century to the board of trustees. Colleges, he wrote, have "character" and a "fixed set of ideas" that the academic community holds. And the character of Trinity is one that makes it "aggressive in its efforts to develop the best interests of society." Essential to the task, he added, was the freedom to do its work. "If Trinity College is to be of any real force in education and in society," he stated emphatically, "it must be free."

Kilgo of course did not know how discerning he was in making the twin issues of social responsibility and academic freedom so prominent in his report to the trustees. In the twentieth century, as the character of the college became more clearly defined, and as its means to accomplish its aims became more stable, Duke University faced new challenges to its tradition of academic freedom.

William Preston Few, president of Trinity College for 14 years and of Duke University for 16 years — a regime that lasted till 1940 — influenced the history of the institution as it is known today more than any other individual. Quiet, scholarly, and seemingly shy, he contrasted sharply with his predecessor and with many other contemporary leaders in higher education. As the university community well knew, however, he had a keen sense of direction, an understanding yet firm administrative manner, and the patience to work quietly behind the scenes and wait for the right moment to voice his ideas. Indeed, when certain people questioned the propriety of the appearance on campus of prominent Socialist, Norman Thomas, in December 1930, President Few moved swiftly and quietly to explain his attitude toward academic freedom and its tradition at the university.

Thomas, then 46 years old, was widely known for his writings and as the Socialist Party candidate for president of the United States. Popular as a campus speaker, he was on a Southern tour which included nearby appearances at North Carolina State College in Raleigh and a mass meeting of textile strikers in Danville, Va. His hastily arranged speech at Duke was sponsored by the Liberal Club, a loosely organized student group. A reporter described his speech as "iconoclastic yet quietly sincere." Henry R. Dwire, director of public relations and alumni affairs, said that it "created no stir on the campus."

Yet within ten days of Thomas's appearance, letters of inquiry about official sponsorship of the speech and the rationale for granting Thomas a platform arrived in the offices of the president and the director of public relations. The *Southern Textile Bulletin*, an influential weekly trade journal attacked Thomas's visit in an editorial entitled "They Honor Norman Thomas." Identifying Thomas as "an advocate of social equality between the races" and "one of those who seek to destroy our Government," the editorial castigated the two universities for giving him a public platform. Duke was singled out for special attention: "As one member of the Duke faculty recently accepted membership upon the National Committee of the notorious American Civil Liberties Union and another....addressed the Foreign Policy Association in New York upon 'Communism's Challenge to Capitalism,' it is easy to name those who brought Norman Thomas to Duke University."

Proud of the distinguished and often young faculty hired to develop the graduate and professional schools, Few took special offense at the textile journal's implication of guilt-by-association. The unnamed professor, a member of the ACLU, was Elbert Russell, friend and former Quaker pastor of President Herbert Hoover, and Dean of Duke's Divinity School. The other was Calvin B. Hoover, professor of economics and recipient of a Guggenheim Fellowship for study in Russia. Moreover, the person who had sent Few a reprint of the editorial was none other than William R. Perkins, chief legal advisor to the late James B. Duke, trustee and vice-chairman of the Duke Endowment, and trustee of the university.

In many ways, President Few had a special obligation to answer Perkins's request for his views on the issue. A native Virginian, Perkins was educated at Washington and Lee and had practiced law in Virginia and New York City principally on behalf of the Duke business interests. Thus he had only limited knowledge of the struggles and strengths of Trinity College in its early years. Few also knew that the personal ties of the Duke family and Trinity College of an earlier era were giving way to new relationships between the benefactors' business partners and the growing university.

> # NORMAN THOMAS IS BROUGHT HERE BY LIBERAL CLUB
>
> ## Well-Known Leader of Socialist Party to Speak at Duke December 6
>
> ## NOTED SOCIAL THINKER
>
> ### Has Achieved Recognition as Author; Was Presidential Candidate of Party in 1928

Chronicle *notice of 1930 speech that initiated a behind-the-scenes debate on the role of a university between President Few and the late J. B. Duke's business associates.*

In a six-page letter to Perkins, Few spoke carefully and frankly to the question of academic freedom. He pointed out that rather than an atheist and advocate of free love, as the editorial claimed, Thomas was a "Presbyterian preacher, A. B. of Princeton and B. D. of Union....in all probability sincerely interested in the well-being of mankind." Since Few had been in Atlanta on business at the time of Thomas's speech, and since Thomas had not been invited by the university, Few had known nothing of Thomas's appearance.

"If I had been here I think I should have been obliged to let the matter go as it did go," said Few, "namely, just to ignore it and let him have his say." Of the "allusion with unfair implications" to Professor Hoover, Few said that Hoover had "an unfavorable view" of the probable outcome of the experiment going on in Russia, but that even if he had felt the experiment would succeed, "it is the part of wisdom not to ignore facts but to look them in the face and prepare ourselves to meet them."

Few's main point had a direct correlation to the issues of the Bassett Affair and the manner of its resolution. Commenting that there had always been "danger in the old South of the prostitution of higher education by politics," he added that "in North Carolina, at least, we have won that fight." Pointing out that many had feared that organized religion might handicap the development of a university such as Duke, he stated that he had never seen from any church such "unfairness and little-mindedness like this which you call to my attention." Instead, he said, it surprised him that the greatest danger came from groups interested mostly in industry and economics. "Publications like the *Southern Textile Bulletin* with its heat, misrepresentation, and wholesale unfairness, and the climate of opinion such as it cultivates were the ruin of the old South," Few warned. "If they are to have influence in our day they will bring our civilization also to ruin."

The president then defended the "careful selection" of faculty in "highly inflammable" subjects like government, economics, sociology, psychology and philosophy" stating that they must be permitted to "proclaim truth as they see it." Clearly, he said, "it is the business of Duke University to hear both sides of all questions." Eloquently appealing for support of his concept of "university-mindedness," Few outlined Duke University's unique opportunity in the South in 1930 to contribute to building "a civilization of really great and enduring qualities." Few said that the university would need all the power, vision and wisdom it could get, and "we shall especially need the open mind and willingness to give a fair hearing to every well-meaning man." As Trinity College evolved into a complex university ample opportunities arose to explain and defend the new role of an aspiring major research university.

Sentimental Journey: Students Help Launch the Big Band Era

Before World War I popular college rhythmic music was called ragtime. Then jazz took over until about 1935 when swing reigned. At Duke music also was an enjoyable way of earning ones way through school. Live student dance bands were popular, each with its following much like athletic teams.

Even though college students and some form of music are inseparable, administrative authorities have not always sanctioned dancing or even student tastes in music. Trinity students first had a String Band and later a Mandolin Club but they played only concerts or for square dances which were becoming increasingly out of favor. Then as one student put it, dancing ceased altogether because "a dance during President Kilgo's administration (1894–1910) would have been comparable to inviting Lucifer himself to give a chapel talk and stay for dinner." However, social norms gradually changed along with administrations, and fraternities and sororities began having dances off campus. Then in February, 1927 the college actually approved a Junior Prom at the new downtown Washington Duke

Student band leaders Johnny Long '35, on the left, and Les Brown '36, on the right, who went on to fame during the Big Band Era.

Hotel. By the late 1930s dances averaged three a week from unpretentious YMCA or YWCA Open Houses, to twice-yearly well decorated formal Co-Ed Balls. Nationally well known bands were welcomed on campus including that of Jimmie Lunceford, the popular African American band leader who performed at the Pan Hellenic Dance in 1938.

However, the mainstay of the campus social scene was the local student band. Most often the bands had elected officers, shared profits, and were identified by a particular musical style and well-known leader. Usually the two most favored bands played nightly during dinnertime on East and West campuses. One band would play in the Union Ballroom, now the Faculty Commons, on West, and the other would play in the Ark on East, and they would alternate monthly. The administration provided free meals as compensation for the band members. The band's primary income, at the top price of $300 a night, came from weekend dances within commuting distance. On holidays, they played throughout the East Coast, and if really successful, some bands earned extended summer tours at popular vacation resorts. On occasion a few bands traveled in Europe over the summer earning sea passage playing on ocean liners.

Some of the student bands were known as the Swing Kings, Blue Dukes, Blue Imps, Grand Dukes, and the D-Men, a play on the popular name for FBI agents, G-Men. The most frequently used name was the Blue Devils which passed from its originator "Jelly" Leftwich in 1926 to four successors with Les Brown last directing a band with that name in 1936. Perhaps the most surprising band director was a star football player, Nick Laney, who was known as the "Croonin Halfback." The longest-lasting name was the Duke Ambassadors which was used until 1964 and is the precursor to today's Duke Jazz Ensemble. Of the student frontmen only Les Brown was a "schooled musician" having graduated from Ithaca Conservatory of Music before entering Duke.

Though strictly amateurs primarily seeking a good time and college expenses, the bands were quite serious about their work. The elected officers, usually a business manager, treasurer, and director, had clearly defined duties. The constitution of Johnny Long's Duke Collegians required the eleven signers to return to school and stay together until June 1, 1935 to allow those eligible to graduate. Pledging to improve the dance band both "musically and morally" they required courtesy among themselves and to the public, and demanded gentlemanly conduct during rehearsals and engagements. Fines were levied for drinking within five hours of rehearsals and performances, and for tardiness and unkempt uniforms.

Johnny Long and Les Brown had the most successful musical careers of the Duke band leaders. Johnny Long had his own band into the 1960s and he shared in directing a band until his death in 1972. His most successful single recording was "Shanty in Old Shanty Town" which sold over 4 million records. Critics claimed Long never developed a distinctive style, a prerequisite to break into the so-called top ten. Instead Long concentrated on staying power preferring to provide the best dance music in the prevailing style of the changing decades.

Les Brown and his Band of Renown is still performing in the 1990s, primarily in California. His signature recording is "Sentimental Journey" and he is best known today as the band of Bob Hope. Brown has performed at Duke with regularity, often for formal dances and lawn concerts on the main quad when Joe College weekend was an annual occurrence. He appeared as guest conductor with Paul Jeffrey and the Duke Jazz Ensemble in 1985 and his entire band played a benefit performance in 1987 for the Les Brown Endowment he established at the university.

Returning alumni from the 1930s and Big Band Era fondly recall "those warm fall and spring evenings, sitting on the grass outside the Union and listening to those favorite tunes as played by Nick Laney, Johnny Long, or Les Brown—'Carolina Moon,' 'Carolina in the Morning,' and of course 'Dear Old Duke.'"

Les Brown's band dressed for a performance. Brown, fifth from the left, and his colleagues earned college expenses by playing for weekend dances on the east coast.

Coach Wallace Wade Set a Tone for Combining Athletics and Academics _____

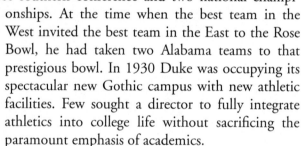

Rival coaches Wallace Wade (1892–1986) of Duke, on the left, and Bob Neyland of Tennessee, on the right, shake hands after a football game.

President William P. Few's practice in staffing the new university was to seek advice from established scholars and respected administrators. Early in 1930, he had William H. Wannamaker, chief academic officer and chair of the faculty committee on athletics, write William Wallace Wade, football coach at the University of Alabama, for a confidential recommendation for a football coach and director of athletics. Then thirty-nine years old, Wade was at the top of his profession having built Alabama's football program and with it respect for southern football as being among the nation's elite. In seven years Wade's teams had a record of 51–13–3 with three southern conference and two national championships. At the time when the best team in the West invited the best team in the East to the Rose Bowl, he had taken two Alabama teams to that prestigious bowl. In 1930 Duke was occupying its spectacular new Gothic campus with new athletic facilities. Few sought a director to fully integrate athletics into college life without sacrificing the paramount emphasis of academics.

In response, Wade dutifully recommended two individuals but in a surprise ending, he stated that he had one more year on his contract and if Duke would be willing to wait, he would like to talk about the position himself. Confidential negotiations proceeded until Wade accepted the Duke position. Ironically his last year at Alabama produced yet another undefeated season with a Rose Bowl victory and his third national championship. Speculation was rampant as to why he would leave at such a time. It was rumored that a salary higher than that of President Few enticed him but in reality his salary did not exceed that of several administrators.

Success soon followed at Duke as well. Within three years Duke football improved with seasons of 5–3–2, 7–3, and 9–1 and a conference championship in 1933. Duke had the first All-American player in North Carolina in Fred Crawford in 1932 and 1933. In sixteen years Wade had an impressive record of 110 wins, 36 losses and 7 ties with seven conference championships and national rankings from first to fourth by various rating systems in 1938, 1939 and 1941. The "Iron Duke" team of 1938 was undefeated, untied and unscored upon before a heartbreaking 7–3 loss in Duke's first Rose Bowl game when Southern California scored in the last minute of play. Duke hosted the Rose Bowl in 1942 because of the surprise military attack at Pearl Harbor on December 7, 1941 for the only time it has ever been played away from California. Although favored, Duke lost to Oregon State 20 to 16. Wade took responsiblity for the defeat saying the myriad details of being host distracted him. But the team played its worst game of the year. It was greatly disappointed with the relocation since it lost a glamorous trip to California and it had to practice in Durham over Christmas vacation as well. Wade coached twenty-six All-American players at Duke with eight joining him in the National Football Hall of Fame.

Also employed as Director of Physical Education and Intramurals, Wade implemented a program that the *Chronicle* reported had over ninety percent of undergraduate men taking part in at least one sports activity. Basketball and boxing were the most popular sports. Physical education courses enrolled almost seven hundred men with tennis and swimming attracting the most interest. The women's physical education and athletic programs were administered separately through the undergraduate Woman's College.

A not insignificant footnote to Wade's career relates to the racial integration of football. Even though a native southerner and coach in a segregated system of education, Wade had no qualms about playing integrated teams. He had been a teammate of Fritz Pollard, an African American All-American, at Brown University when they played together in the Rose Bowl in 1916. In 1938 Duke had an away game at Syracuse which had an outstanding dark skinned player named Wilmeth Sidat-Singh. While some Southern schools asked that Sidat-Singh not be in the line up against them and their wishes were honored, Wade made no such request. When queried Wade said "We want to beat them at their best" Duke did, 21–0. In 1950 a visiting team from Pittsburgh brought the first African American player to play an integrated game in North Carolina. President Edens and Wade issued a press release welcoming the team to Durham. The game was played without incident on or off the field.

Wade retired from coaching in 1950 to become commissioner of the Southern Conference. In 1967 the university named its football stadium after Wallace Wade. Despite being in five Halls of Fame, he considered the naming of the stadium his greatest honor. He was always proud and amused when introductions to strangers usually brought the comment "You're the man Duke stadium is named after!" He continued to live in Durham raising cattle on a farm in Bahama until his death at age 94 in 1986. In his eulogy President Terry Sanford remembered Wade as a man who "held presence, commanded attention and demanded excellence." His players held him in awe. At the fifty year reunion of the Durham Rose Bowl game, after Wade's death, team members were overheard debating whether or not to wear a coat and tie to the stadium on a very hot Saturday afternoon.

Someone said "The Old Man," (his players affectionate name for him, obviously used behind his back), "would want us to wear a coat and tie." They did.

Why did Wade leave Alabama for Duke? He steadfastly refused to answer that question until an interview with a sport's historian late in his life. It was not the challenge of reviving another dormant football program. Nor was it for the money. He welcomed the opportunity to direct a total athletic program including intramural activities for all students. His philosophy regarding athletics and academics fit perfectly with that of the Duke administration. But having experienced the difference between programs at private and state universities since he was an assistant coach at Vanderbilt before going to Alabama, above all, Wade wanted the greater freedom from interference he believed a private university provided. His surprise decision was an excellent match for Wade, for Duke and for football.

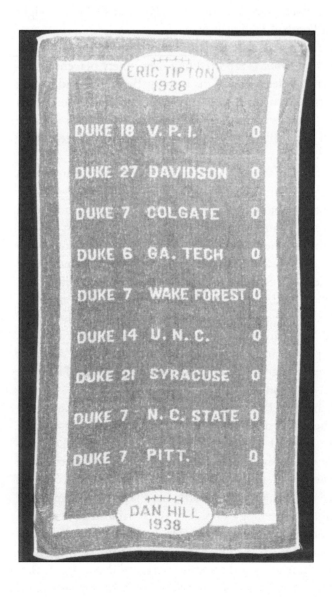

The university's most famous football team was called the Iron Dukes for its defensive prowess. The term for Duke's first Rose Bowl team is now used by the university's primary support group for athletics.

Edmund M. Cameron: The Man and the Stadium

When each home basketball game begins with the announcement "Welcome to Cameron Indoor Stadium" those assembled are enjoying a game in the building named after Edmund McCullough Cameron and they are reminded of one of the university's most revered coach-administrators. Cameron called the naming of the building on January 22, 1972 "his most cherished honor." An added bonus was a Duke upset of the nationally third ranked University of North Carolina Tar Heels, 76 to 74, in the first game in the renamed arena. That Eddie Cameron would so highly value the renaming of the Indoor Stadium demonstrates his affection for the university. It also apparently eclipses a lifetime of superlative accomplishments as a player, coach and administrator that earned him induction into five Halls of Fame. Altogether he was inducted into the National Football, Atlantic Coast Conference Sports Writers, Duke University and North Carolina and Virginia Halls of Fame.

Cameron's active participation in Duke athletics spanned forty-six years from 1926 to 1972, the second longest tenure in the school's history. However, his unofficial contribution continued sixteen more years after retirement until his death in 1988 at age 86. He held more different positions and exercised greater responsibility in athletics on and off campus than any other Duke administrator.

Born near Pittsburgh, Pennsylvania in 1902, Cameron won honors in several sports at Culver Military Academy in Indiana and Washington and Lee University in Virginia. At Washington and Lee he was captain of both the basketball and football teams and he tied for national scoring honors in football. When Duke hired the W and L football coach, Jimmy DeHart, Cameron followed him to Durham to coach the freshman team. He proved to be an excellent coach and popular member of the university community and when Wallace Wade was enticed to Duke from Alabama, administrators urged him to retain Cameron. Cameron became backfield coach, scout and recruiter for Wade with the added responsibility of head basketball coach from 1929 to 1942.

While "Cap" Card is credited with introducing basketball in 1905, Eddie Cameron's success built the popularity for the sport as we know it today. Cameron's first two teams surprised many by making it to the finals of the Southern Conference tournament as a new member of the league. Duke also had its first All-American basketball player in Bill Werber. Cameron had a fourteen-year record of 226–99 with conference championships in 1938, 1941 and 1942. The team also reached the championship game four other times. In an astonishing move, Duke built the largest basketball arena south of the Palestra in Philadelphia in 1940. Ironically, Cameron's contribution in football contributed to the basketball arena as well because Duke used money earned in the school's first Rose Bowl appearance in 1939 to partially finance the construction of the dramatic new indoor stadium. Cameron coached the dedicatory game and first victory in the stadium on January 6, 1940 when Duke defeated Princeton University 36 to 27.

Cameron's record was equally impressive when he became head football coach in 1942 when Wallace Wade entered military service in World War II. In four years Cameron's teams won three conference championships while compiling a record of 25–11–1. Eight of the losses were to service teams which were more like professional teams in the war years. Cameron's teams lost only one game to the

Eddie Cameron's (1902–1988) active participation in Duke athletics spanned forty-six years.

Big Four in the state and he never lost to North Carolina even defeating them twice in the 1943 season. The 1943 team led the nation in scoring with 335 points and in defense giving up just 34 points in nine games. However, the climax of Cameron's football career came with Duke's first post season victory when Duke defeated Alabama, 29 to 26, in the 1945 Sugar Bowl. Cameron became permanent Director of Physical Education and Athletics in 1946 when Wade returned and resumed coaching football.

Cameron was one of the nation's most influential athletic administrators. He was a founder of the Atlantic Coast Conference. He chaired the basketball committee of the Southern and ACC conferences for decades where he steadfastly supported the crowning of a champion by an end-of-the-year tournament. He also served on the selection committee for the national Football Hall of Fame and the governing committee of the Olympics.

However, he took the greatest pride in the changing face of Duke athletics. He was most excited about opening new facilities such as the move from Hanes Football Field on East Campus to the new 35,000 seat stadium on West, or the move from Card Gym to the new indoor stadium for basketball. But he was equally pleased with the planning and opening of a long awaited 18 hole golf course, expanded baseball and track facilities, and the construction of a new indoor swimming pool.

Eddie Cameron's funeral filled the Duke Chapel. Even though former players, coaches, administrators, colleagues and family traveled from around the nation to pay respect, he had requested that the service be simple and brief. He wanted no eulogy. The starting five of the then number one ranked Duke basketball team carried his casket from the chapel. Nevertheless, there were individual reminiscences aplenty. Vic Bubas, a former Duke basketball coach whom Cameron hired, noted that Cameron seldom was around the locker room when the team won. However, when the losses were tough, he always showed up. Said Bubas, "He was a very compassionate man. That set him apart from many others." Cameron's tenure began at the time of transition from Trinity College to Duke University. His leadership and personality marked the institution's athletic program for over fifty years contributing like no other to the success and respect enjoyed by the university.

Fields of Trees: Clarence Korstain Built a Forest and School and Researchers Are Still Coming _____

Clarence F. Korstain (1889–1968) came to Duke in 1930 to manage its extensive forest and later launch the School of Forestry as its first Dean.

In September, 1938, the School of Forestry opened with nine faculty and twenty-one students from thirteen states and four foreign countries. With meticulous planning, the hiring of an impressive faculty and an emphasis on research and service, the Forestry School was not unlike the professional schools of law, divinity, medicine and nursing that preceded it. Yet it was different in that a School of Forestry had not been mentioned in the Duke indenture in 1924. Instead it evolved out of the acquisition of a sizable tract of land, some 5,000 acres by 1925, and the desire of be of service to the region. As the plans for the new university came to fruition in the 1920s, President William Preston Few was urged to create a strong, independent forestry school, based on the Yale model, that would focus on research and forest management in the southern environment.

A careful planner, Few sought the advice of many. Soon Clarence F. Korstian, silviculturist at the Appalachian Forest Experiment Station of the U.S. Forest Service in Asheville, was stopping in Durham on trips to the coast to survey lowland forests. Unknowingly, he was being evaluated, and much to his surprise at the end of one meeting, he was offered the position of manager of the Duke Forest with the expectation that he would develop a curriculum in forestry in due time. Typically, Few had worked cautiously, behind the scenes in selecting Korstian, and time proved that Few made the right choice. Korstian accepted the offer, excited by the challenge and grateful for the opportunity to spend more time with his growing family and less in extensive travel.

Age forty-one when he came to Duke in 1930, Korstian had had most appropriate and varied work experiences as preparation for managing a forest, as well as the best academic training the field then had to offer. A son of pioneers in Nebraska, Korstian knew the necessity of hard physical labor for survival. He grew up living in a prairie schooner and sod house as his father farmed in the harsh midwestern environment. Drought, or "the dryness" as Korstian called it, and economic depressions forced the family to relocate more than once. Given the opportunity to attend college through the state land grant university, Korstian elected to major in forestry because of part-time work in a nursery. Because the department at the University of Nebraska was so small, Korstian later attributed two lessons he acted on at Duke to his undergraduate experience. He knew the value of interdisciplinary study, especially between forestry and botany, and he believed if one could not win support for a strong viable program, it was not worth stringing it along. Korstian worked as a timber surveyor and fire fighter before earning his Ph.D. degree in 1926 at the prestigious forestry program at Yale. He had a distinguished career in the U. S. Forest Service, working in Washington, California, New Mexico and Utah before being assigned to a new station in North Carolina. He also served on the editorial board of the interdisciplinary professional journal, *Ecology*. Few knew Clarence Korstian was unique, having the right combination of academic credentials, professional contacts and collegial respect.

Korstian had strong convictions about forest management. At Duke, he wanted a research and demonstration forest with the capacity to earn financial support through timber management. The Duke forest was ideal with an average elevation of 300 to 600 feet and very little rock and swampland. It had a large variety of hardwoods and a secondary growth of shortleaf and loblolly pine. It was well suited for research in support of southern furniture and paper industries. Korstian wisely utilized New Deal programs such as the Civilian Conservation Corps, the Federal Emergency Relief Administration and the National Youth Administration to employ laborers, including students, in building roads and bridges and in controlling erosion and planting new trees. He demonstrated Duke's commitment to research by gaining membership in the International Union of Forest Research Organizations within a year. The Duke Forest was the first in the south and only the seventh in the United States to participate in that international program.

The forest was clearly an adjunct to the classroom as well. Korstian likened the forest to a forestry curriculum as the hospital to the medical school. Gradually faculty were employed in forest soils, utilization, measurement, wood technology and silviculture, and botany professors assisted in forest pathology and plant physiology. A department of forestry was formally organized in 1934 before it became a School of Forestry in 1938, perhaps the first such school of graduate education only in the south.

Korstian later reported that he learned of being named dean through a telephone call from his wife to Atlanta where he was on business. She had read about it in a newspaper article reporting on actions taken by the board of trustees. Korstian was not surprised. It had long been assumed he would direct the new school and he simply stated that Few sometimes acted in that manner. Korstian served as dean until 1957 before retiring in 1959. In recognition of his long, distinguished service to the university and to his profession, the board of trustees named one of the major areas of the Duke Forest the C. F. Korstian Division.

By the 1970s enrollment in forestry programs declined nationwide. The Duke program was well positioned to adapt to changing circumstances. In 1974 a Master of Environmental Management degree was approved and the school was renamed the School of Forestry and Environmental Studies. The curriculum began to shift toward environmental science building on the well established Duke tradition of interdisciplinary study. In 1991 the long standing program at the Duke Marine Laboratory on the coast was incorporated creating the university's newest professional school, the School of the Environment under the direction of Dean Norman L. Christensen. Its curriculum is comprised of five areas of emphasis: forest resource management; resource ecology; environmental toxicology, chemistry, and risk assessment; biohazard science; water and air resources; resource economics and policy; and coastal environmental management. By planning appropriately, students in the school of the environment can also earn, concurrent degrees of master of business administration, or master of arts in public policy sciences or juris doctor in environmental law.

Truly, perhaps uniquely, interdisciplinary, Duke offers undergraduate and graduate degrees in several areas of study related to natural resources and the environment. In recognition of Duke's effort to teach problem-solving skills in an increasingly complicated subject area and its novel approach to environmental study, business executive Peter Nicholas and his wife, Virginia Lilly Nicholas, alumni of the class of 1964, donated $20 million to the School of the Environment on Founders' Weekend in December, 1995. In recognition of the gift which is second only to that of founder James B. Duke, the board of trustees renamed the professional school the Nicholas School of the Environment.

One wonders what Clarence F. Korstian would think about the evolution of the School of Forestry. Given his background and life-long commitment to the study of ecology, he probably would be nostalgic about his day-to-day work in forestry, but he would fully understand and applaud the transition to a new curriculum and the educational efforts to meet current problems in the environment.

A platform for research in the 8,000-acre Duke forest.

Duke Opens Doors to Jewish Émigré Scholars

The volume in the records of President William P. Few is marked Strictly Confidential. It is dated 1936 and titled *List of Displaced German Scholars*. In content, it consists of over 1,600 of the briefest of biographical sketches of victims of political persecution in Germany. Specifically the purpose of the compilation was to assist in finding employment for "Jewish scholars; scholars with Jewish antecedents or those connected with Jews by marriage; and non-Jewish scholars whose convictions made them unacceptable to the German Government." Arranged by academic discipline, one can easily identify, for example, 102 psychologists, 104 sociologists or 197 theologians. The list seems to go on and on including the now familiar names of Einstein, Lewin, Barth and Tillich. No researcher from a university where academic freedom is valued can peruse the volume without some emotional reaction. Each listing represents the uprooting of family and the interruption of teaching and research. Both men and women and established and promising scholars are included.

At least five individuals employed by Duke are listed in the volume. That Duke would employ so many émigrés is perhaps surprising because despite obvious academic advantages and humanitarian appeal, such action was nevertheless controversial. The organizers of the placement service were concerned about anti-Semitism. Religious prejudice, however, was often less a problem than anti-foreign attitudes. During the Great Depression, as salaries were cut and research funds lost, many native-born professors and administrators resented limited funds going to foreign refugees. As organizations began locating scholars, the South, as a region, was perhaps the slowest area to offer assistance. Among institutions, prestigious Harvard University was conspicuously absent in some of the early initiatives.

At Duke, President Few responded to the crisis immediately. Nationally, the most prominent organization offering assistance was the Emergency Committee in Aid of Displaced German Scholars, based in New York City. When its assistant secretary, Edward R. Murrow, sent a general appeal to college and university presidents in November, 1933, Few responded on the day of receipt. He wrote, "I shall be very glad to have a

William Stern (1871–1938), the renowned psychologist who developed the IQ test, taught at Duke from 1934 to 1938.

list of available men for consideration." Within three weeks, Few submitted seven names in preferential order, closing by saying, "We shall be very happy to have one, or if possible even more, of these men to sojourn with us." He added that if none of those identified were available he would submit another list.

The program of the Emergency Committee offered decided advantages for Duke. Distinguished scholars were available to help in the staffing of new or expanding academic programs. And they were available at no expense for the New York committee and the Rockefeller Foundation shared in paying all of the émigrés salary. Later the flood of refugees and limited available funds necessitated a more restrictive policy. Scholars were placed with salary paid only for a limited term, and then only if the institution guaranteed a permanent position or tenure. The change did not lessen Few's enthusiasm. With active encouragement from William McDougall, Chairman of the Psychology Department, and others, Few employed German scholars both with and without the assistance of the Emergency Committee.

In 1934 Few was elated to have an acceptance from his first choice, William Stern, the psychologist who developed the IQ test. Upon renewal of Stern's contract Few wrote Murrow, "Stern has been quite acceptable. He has given a course of lectures in German and at the last one he received a great ovation, including flowers." Unfortunately Few had to write the New York office in April, 1938 that Stern had died unexpectedly. "We had all come to be attached to him and to Mrs. Stern," Few noted. "Our whole community is deeply distressed by his sudden death."

Walter Kempner arrived in the Medical School as Associate in Medicine and Physiology in the same year as Stern. He came with the assistance of Frederic M. Hanes, Professor of Medicine, and his research established the reversibility of major disease processes through dietary control. The general populace knows Kempner as the originator of the Rice Diet which established Durham's reputation as a renowned diet center.

Hertha Sponer (1895–1968), characterized by a colleague as one of the three most respected women physicists in the world, came to Duke in 1936.

With the arrival of Hertha Sponer in February, 1936, Duke acquired one of the foremost women scientists in Europe. At her employment, Few ignored the advice of a prominent American physicist who urged him not to weaken his developing department with the addition of a woman. Sponer, who was married to the Nobel Prize winning physicist, James Franck, taught at Duke until her retirement in 1966.

Herbert von Beckerath arrived in 1935 with a dual appointment at Duke and the University of North Carolina. He was considered the foremost authority in Germany on industrial policy and organization. Howard W. Odum sought his expertise for the interdisciplinary approach he was developing in sociology at UNC and Duke employed him as a professor in economics and political science. As a Protestant, von Beckerath fled Germany for political reasons. He taught solely at Duke from 1938 until his retirement in 1955.

The last émigré employed through the Emergency Committee was Lothar Nordheim, a physicist, who began teaching in the fall of 1937. When Purdue University could not continue his salary, his temporary grant was transferred to Duke on condition of permanent employment. Nordheim joined the Manhattan Project in 1943 before working on the thermonuclear weapons programs at Oak Ridge and Los Alamos. He left Duke for the atomic division of General Dynamics in 1956.

The last of the émigrés to join the faculty was Fritz London who came from Oxford University in 1938. He was contacted and employed by Paul M. Gross, Chairman of the Department of Chemistry. Trained in philosophy, mathematics, and physics, London is perhaps the most distinguished and creative faculty member in the history of the university. After early publications in philosophy and quantum chemistry, he began a life-long investigation of the peculiar phenomena, associated with extremely low temperatures, of superconductivity and superfluidity. London won the prestigious Lorentz Medal, given by the Royal Dutch Academy of Sciences, in 1953, the same year he was named James B. Duke Professor of Chemistry. At the time of his premature death in 1954, he was considered to be a leading candidate for the Nobel Prize. Later Nobel Prize winners have acknowledged that their research was based on the earlier works of Fritz London.

All of the men and women who came to Duke from Germany in the 1930s contributed significantly to their academic disciplines and enriched the community with their presence. All undoubtedly had a poignant personal story much of which they probably kept to themselves. History has proven that the effort expended at relocating by both the displaced scholars and those who assisted them was well worth the sacrifice.

Fritz London (1907–1954) came to Duke in chemistry and physics in 1938. In 1953 he won the prestigious Lorentz Medal given by the Royal Dutch Academy of Sciences.

December, 1941: Duke Prepares for War and Football _____

"Sunday used to be a day of rest and quiet," lamented the *Chronicle* on December 9, 1941. That sentiment was stated because the campus mood swung widely as the month unfolded. Two Sunday's previously, the announcement of Oregon State's invitation to Duke to play in the Rose Bowl had set off one of the wildest celebrations in Duke history. In anticipation, Duke students were crowded around every teletype machine in town. Upon confirmation of the acceptance, one long continuous parade of cars circled Main Street between the campus and the Court House. The celebration over Duke's second Rose Bowl appearance in four years was only slightly diminished when the women had to return to their dorms at their 11:00 p.m. curfew. The most frequently wired Western Union message was "Send Pasadena money" when a repeat of the popular 1939 "Blue Devil Special" was announced. Round-trip railroad fare with Pullman accommodations, including a side trip to the Grand Canyon, hotel fare, and game ticket cost only $181.81.

Sunday evening, December 7, found many of the same students at the same teletype machines in a much more somber mood. Students had rushed downtown when the Herald-Sun Extra Edition proclaiming "Hitler's War Explodes In World Conflict As Japanese Attack U. S." appeared on campus. Then the most frequent questions were "Where is Pearl Harbor?" and "What is the status of the draft legislation under review in Washington?"

The *Chronicle* writer further commented that he hoped the next Sunday would not bring the announcement that Pasadena was bombed. His premonition was close because fearing just such an eventuality, the next Sunday's news announced the canceling of the Rose Bowl game. However, Duke University's offer to host the game was accepted setting off another celebration, although a decidedly quieter one. The overriding concern was how to get ready for such a unique event in just eighteen days.

Not everyone was elated over the dramatic turn of events. The football team was disappointed over the loss of their trip to glamorous California. With war declared, many members were not at all pleased at the prospect of Christmas being spent away from family in preparation for a game in Durham.

While *Chronicle* headlines outline the rapidly changing events, a closer inspection of articles reveals that not all events were unquestioned or unanticipated. Despite the fact that the football team was undefeated and untied, ranked second in the nation, and the highest scoring team in Wade's tenure, conjecture over a bowl bid did not dominate the news.

A campus editorial clearly placed football in perspective. Citing belief in a proper balance between athletics and academics, the paper declared the "sports pages are not the section in which Duke University or any great university needs publicity." Universities justly become great, the editorial stated, when they receive publicity on science, editorial and book review pages, and when national publications examine and criticize their research. Stating that the mighty Blue Devils had brought credit to the school, the editorial concluded "If Duke is to have a highly publicized football team, it MUST have a nationally recognized medical center, law clinic, forestry school, engineering college and undergraduate school famous for its high scholastic standards. Otherwise, the school will be known by the epithet 'football college.'"

Neither were students oblivious to unfolding world events. In an eerily accurate editorial appearing just two days before the surprise attack at Pearl Harbor, a columnist wrote "bowl invitations, dances, plays, and approaching Christmas holidays all obscure the unpleasant fact America is on the very brink of war. January 1 will see Duke men in blue football uniform playing in the Rose Bowl. It may also find other Duke men in blue naval uniforms fighting a war."

Once the shock of declared war settled on campus, students faced reality quickly. After an initial rush to enlist, the predominant sentiment was to stay in school. Noting America was famous for winning wars and losing peace conferences, student leaders emphasized that colleges were a vital part of a nation at war. After all, what better place was there for future leaders to learn calm interpretations of events in the face of mass propaganda. To those tempted to party away

Marine and Navy uniforms predominated on campus during World War II.

their last semester before the draft, the admonition was to have a good record when one returned to graduate after the war.

One editorialist looked the "grim dance of death" in the face and went to the heart of the matter. Instead of the urge to enjoy the present to the fullest, he urged that that intensity be directed towards genuine things. "Indifference and sensual escapism make a poor philosophy with which to face a bayonet," he cautioned. He thought "nothing better could be done than to utilize the remaining days in the ivory tower in finding a true faith."

The transplanted Rose Bowl game was played in Durham on January 1. Borrowed bleachers from UNC and NC State boosted stadium capacity from 35,000 to 55,000 spectators. A flood of East Coast sportswriters descended upon Durham for their first Rose Bowl while only a single writer came from southern California. The heavily favored Duke team lost on a cold, rainy day to an underestimated defensive team that successfully protected an early lead. Coach Wade later stated he spent too much time being host and too little time preparing the team. He also gave the team several days off to go home for Christmas. Nevertheless, the university community and nation had more important concerns to face beginning January 2, 1942.

The Rose Bowl game, played for the only time outside of California, drew 55,000 spectators in a greatly expanded stadium. Duke had three weeks to plan for hosting the game.

_____ "Main Street" at Duke Found in Union West

Today the basement level of Union West houses the offices of Auxiliary Services, the Duke Barbershop, and the Mary Lou Williams Cultural Center. The hallway barely fits an earlier characterization of it as "the university's 'Main Street,' a veritable beehive of activity from early morning until late at night." Before the opening of the Bryan Center student activities and services were centered in the Union Building. The dining halls remain virtually unchanged except for the Faculty Commons which has replaced the Union Ballroom where student dances once were held. Alumni Affairs has moved to the Alumni House on Chapel Drive leaving behind the distinctive Alumni Lounge. But the lower level is no longer "Main Street."

For years the center of West Campus activity was the Union basement "Dope Shop." The unusual name often caused quizzical looks including those of John F. Kennedy who stopped by for a hamburger on the way to a Page Auditorium lecture the night before he announced his candidacy for president of the United States. Years ago "dope" was a Southern slang term for a cola drink, perhaps due

The popular campus "Dope Shop" or soda fountain and grill in the basement of the West Campus Union.

to the belief that Coca-Cola contained a small amount of cocaine. The term was used on campus from at least before World War I when enterprising students opened a shop for candy and tobacco in Epworth and later Aycock dormitories. The most popular drink in the West Campus Dope Shop was a delicious thick milkshake. Quick service was the main appeal, but at various times the store had booths for socializing and a pool table and jukebox as well.

Next door was the University Store selling everything a student needed including school supplies from slide rules to examination "blue books." In September, 1972, male students were surprised to discover items like *Cosmopolitan* and hair spray in "their" store as women moved into West Campus residence halls for the first time. In former years the clothing portion of the store was known as the Haberdashery, a place "with the well dressed university man in mind." Gradually Duke-imprinted items took over as tastes changed and formal attire gave way to more casual dress.

Across the hall the University Bookstore sold course required textbooks only. The extremely cramped quarters necessitated sales of most textbooks at the beginning of each semester in the concourse of Cameron Indoor Stadium where course registration was held.

The old West Campus Post Office in the basement of the Union is now the location of the Mary Lou Williams Center for Black Culture.

The Barbershop carried on a campus tradition dating from 1912 when the college first employed two experienced barbers. In 1941 the West Campus shop kept six barbers and two shoeshine boys busy. It too changed with the times employing the first African American barber in 1969 and the first woman in 1972. The slogan "where friends meet for better service" remains true today as this part of "Main Street" continues in the same location.

Often visited twice a day, the post office is probably the most frequented place on campus. The Union Post Office had over 900 individual boxes where the Mary Lou Williams Cultural Center is now located. The West Campus branch also served 500 boxes each in the hospital and on East Campus. In 1934 the downtown train schedule permitted five deliveries and pick ups of mail on campus per day. Anticipated news and cookies from home, letters from girlfriends (and after 1972, boyfriends), and grades via self-addressed post cards kept the path to the post office well worn.

A bank, a laundry and the campus mail office also contributed to constant traffic. Intermingled from time to time were offices for the *Chanticleer*, the *Archive* (the literary magazine), the *Chronicle*, and the Student Government Association. After a walk down the Union "Main Street" it is easy to appreciate the Bryan Center. Within a week of the opening of the new campus center in 1982, it was hard to imagine that the campus had not always been blessed with so much space for campus and student services.

Russian Studies Program Has Distinguished History

When the Honorable Jack F. Matlock, Ambassador to the Soviet Union, spoke at Founders' Day in 1990 it marked the return to campus of a distinguished alumnus. In the course of his remarks he revealed that three section heads and one deputy section head of his staff were also Duke graduates. He hastened to add, however, that each person earned his position in his own right and that none was appointed through favoritism due to old school ties. This remarkable convergence of Duke graduates in a key legation at a pivotal time in history poses the question of the education that prepared them for their careers in diplomatic service. The early history of Russian studies at Duke is an intriguing story.

Professor John Shelton Curtiss (1899–1983) taught Russian history from 1945 to 1969.

In 1938, Theodore Ropp joined the history faculty as a specialist in military and French history. The popular, young professor suggested to his chairman, William T. Laprade, that he would like to teach Russian history, a course he had at Harvard. Laprade who had been at Duke since 1909, was one of the major architects of the transition from college to university. With a keen judge of talent and a broad vision of curriculum, Laprade readily agreed to the adding of Russian history. Ropp's undergraduate survey course, taught in 1939–40, proved a success attracting about one hundred students.

The tumultuous war years soon scrambled the entire curriculum with major emphasis directed toward required courses in military training. Nevertheless, Laprade remembered the appeal of the initial course in Russian history. The catalogue for 1945–46 lists Associate Professor John S. Curtiss as offering two courses: a survey in Russian history for undergraduates and "Russia in the Twentieth Century" for graduate students. The employment of Curtiss probably represents the first full-time position exclusively in Russian history for a southern university.

In hiring Curtiss, Duke employed one of only three scholars who had earned a Ph.D. at the developing prestigious program in Russian studies at Columbia University. Then forty-six years old, Curtiss had taught himself the Russian language, traveled in Russia, and struggled to support a family and earn an advanced degree during the Great Depression. During World War II he helped staff the Russian Division of the Office of Strategic Services, the forerunner of today's CIA. The division's activity was not "cloak and dagger" but primarily supplying an abysmally ignorant military and civilian bureaucracy with basic facts and analysis of Russian history. Curtiss had won national recognition as the recipient of the Herbert Baxter Adams Award of the American Historical Association for the publication of his dissertation as *Church and State in Russia, 1900 to 1917*. He was to have a long tenure at Duke retiring as James B. Duke Professor in 1969. His last books, *The Russian Army Under Nicholas I* and *Russia's Crimean War* were considered by Russian and American critics as among the most outstanding on their subjects.

Conscious that a complete program in Russian studies had to include study of the language, the university employed Thomas G. Winner as Assistant Professor of Russian Language and Culture in 1948. A native of Czechoslovakia, Winner had studied at the University of Prague before earning A.B. and M.A. degrees from Harvard and a Ph.D. from Columbia. His primary research was in the folklore and literature of the nomadic Kazakhs of Central Asia. Winner's courses proved to be popular with an enrollment of about sixty students per semester. In an interview in 1954, he was proud of the kind of success every teacher cherishes. One of his students had gone on for a Ph.D. at Columbia. While at Duke the student had majored in history but he had taken every course both in language and literature that Winner had taught. Clearly Winner had inspired the student who came to Duke from Greensboro, North Carolina. That student was Jack F. Matlock.

Duke's offerings in Russian studies continued to expand. Winner left for the University of Michigan but Bronislas Jezierski and Robert A. Maguire joined the department at the time the 1958 catalogue was listing the first major in Russian. Increasing demand in the history department resulted in the employment of Warren Lerner in 1961 and Martin A. Miller in 1970 as the specialists in Soviet Russia. While courses in economics and political science had incorporated study of the Soviet economy and government, a major addition to the faculty occurred in 1963 with the arrival of Wladyslaw W. Kulski as James B. Duke Professor of Political Science. Kulski, trained in law, had a distinguished career as a Polish diplomat before teaching in the United States after World War II. This expansion in Russian studies was made possible by a gift from Doris Duke. Jerry F. Hough replaced Kulski at his retirement in 1973.

Duke also has a notable list of faculty in government service including Calvin B. Hoover in economics, E. Malcolm Carroll in history, and R. Taylor Cole in political science. Among the diplomatic corps George V. Allen (Trinity '24) retired with the permanent rank of Career Ambassador after serving thirty years in the foreign service and as Assistant Secretary of State and Director of the USIA. Trustee George McGhee served as Ambassador to Germany and Angier Biddle Duke served as Ambassador to El Salvador, Spain, Denmark, and Morocco, as well as Chief of Protocol for Presidents John F. Kennedy and Lyndon B. Johnson. One should not be surprised to discover university graduates in diplomatic service for mentors in the classroom and role models in the foreign service have inspired generations of students.

Debate Team Creates Controversy During the McCarthy Era _____

The question of academic freedom on campus is a recurring one despite the clear precedent created by the Bassett Affair at Trinity College in 1903. In the 1930s debate was generated by appearances of Socialist Norman Thomas on campus, and in the 1960s Duke became involved in an indirect, although positive, manner when the North Carolina legislature imposed a speaker-ban law on state institutions of higher education.

During the Cold War after World War II, several occasions arose when the university benefited from its tradition of academic freedom. One such incident, the appearance of Joseph C. Wetherby, assistant professor of English and director of debating at Duke, on Edward R. Murrow's CBS television program "See It Now," resulted in nationwide publicity. Professor Wetherby courageously defended the right of intercollegiate debaters to argue the officially adopted topic of the Speech Association of America, "Resolved: That the United States should extend diplomatic recognition to the Communist government of China."

In preparation for competition, Edwin Chapman, Jr., a freshman from Newport News, Va., wrote his congressman, Representative Edward J. Robeson, Jr.,

Joseph C. Wetherby (1910–1976) taught English and directed Duke Debate from 1947 to 1976. He is pictured on the left with debate team member James Harbison.

requesting information relative to the nationally selected topic. Robeson promptly replied, expressing amazement "that such a topic...was even seriously considered by any group of persons who are normally intelligent and responsibly informed." He advised Chapman not to debate the positive position "as quotations from your statements may embarrass you for the rest of your life." Stating that it would be a "great favor," he requested the names of the Debate Club faculty advisor at Duke and the members of the National Debating Council. Since Chapman had used only a university address, the congressman presumed he lived in his district but he concluded by expressing an interest in knowing "just where you reside."

In the regional newsletter of Tau Kappa Alpha, the national forensic honor society, Wetherby warned his fellow coaches of possible trouble with the debate topic. Before long, the Associated Press had reported the Duke incident along with a growing nationwide controversy. The biggest story concerned President Eisenhower being questioned about directives from the Secretaries of the Army and Navy forbidding the debate teams at West Point and Annapolis from debating the topic.

Edward R. Murrow devoted time in two programs in November, 1954, to reporting the controversy and defending the right of free discussion and debate. Wetherby appeared on one "See It Now" show with Wayne C. Eubank of the University of New Mexico, president of Tau Kappa Alpha. Immediately after the program, Wetherby began receiving letters and telegrams, mostly favorable toward his position, from throughout the country.

The president of Duke, A. Hollis Edens, understood the significance of the issue, and did not interfere with either the student group or its faculty advisor. He did, however, receive mail on the subject. Especially welcome was the letter from Peter Maas '49, then public relations director of the Crowell-Collier Publishing Company. Wrote Maas: "This is my first alumnus letter written to the university, and perhaps I have been lax in remaining in contact. However, I want to tell you how impressed I was by Duke University's part on the recent Ed Murrow 'See It Now' broadcast.... Duke's position has certainly earned a vote of confidence from me."

Duke's debate team in 1954–55 included 32 members, 12 of whom took part in 7 tournaments and 94 tournament debates. A student member of that debate team, Carl J. Stewart, Jr., does not recall that the controversy had much effect on the team itself. "There's no question that the national sentiment at that time was that we should not extend recognition to Communist China," he says. "But as far as the debating team went, we found it a fascinating topic and turned up lots of articles on both sides of the issue."

Alumnus Ben L. Smith, superintendent of city schools in Greensboro, N. C., forwarded to President Edens copies of a favorable political cartoon and editorial, and took the unprecedented step of inviting students from the Debate Club to present their arguments before a local Kiwanis Club. An editorial in the *Greensboro Daily News* reminded North Carolinians that the university was following a "high tradition...set years ago...by refusing to dismiss Professor John Spencer Bassett because of the clamor raised when he expressed an unpopular view."

Tabling Richard M. Nixon: The 1954 Controversy Over Awarding an Honorary Degree _____

The only public statement, dated April 7, 1954, read "Annually a number of leading men and women are considered as potential recipients of honorary degrees from Duke University. As a time-honored policy of many years standing, the University does not announce the names of those being considered nor the internal, confidential deliberations that may lead to their selection. In keeping with this policy, the University has no further statement to make." That release concerned deliberations that had begun the previous December, been leaked to the national press the day before, and was not to be resolved essentially until a faculty meeting on June 4. At issue was the awarding of an honorary degree to the Vice President of the United States, Richard M. Nixon, Law School graduate, class of 1937.

Today the minutes of the official bodies only hint at the emotion of the debate and the many issues at stake. However, it clearly was a precursor to a similar much more public campus debate twenty-seven years later over the proposed Nixon presidential library at Duke. Both debates exhibited shrewd tactics and strategy and involved the ever-present tension between administrative and faculty authority. The focal point also was one of the most controversial public figures of the time. Nixon had burst on the national political scene in 1946 by defeating a popular five term Democratic congressman with a strident drum beat of anti-Communist, pro-labor charges. In 1950, he then used his highly visible position on the House Committee on Un-American Activities to advantage in a successful, although again controversial, campaign for the United States Senate. His meteoric rise catapulted him to the vice presidential position on the Republican ticket in 1952 where the presidential nominee, Dwight Eisenhower, seriously considered removing him from the ticket because of charges of Nixon's use of a personal "political slush fund." In 1954, the Vice President was the chief Republican party spokesman and self styled "political animal" in the congressional elections at the height of the McCarthy Era. Controversy followed

OUR NEW PREXY
"NOSE" ALL

Caricature of the president of the student Duke Bar Association, Richard M. Nixon, printed on the program of the annual banquet in 1936.

Nixon in 1981 when he was seeking a permanent location for his library in the aftermath of the Watergate scandal and his resignation from the presidency.

At Duke, formal procedures for the selection of recipients of honorary degrees had been in place since 1922, upon the creation of a Joint Committee of Trustees and Faculty on Honorary Degrees. That committee was to report to the General Faculty in the fall with its recommendation "to lie on the table for two weeks." After action by the faculty, the president was to place the recommendations before the board of trustees for final approval at the board's mid-year meeting. Over time refinements were made in the process and certain traditions evolved. For example, requirements were spelled out and the joint committee came to be thought of as a secret committee even though there was no official designation as such. It came to be accepted that the speaker at commencement merited an honorary degree as well.

On January 14, 1954 the Joint Committee reported three names for honorary degrees, including Nixon's, to the General Faculty. Final consideration was to follow at its next meeting. On February 11, with a noticeable increase in attendance, two names were approved unanimously without debate, but it was moved that Nixon's nomination be tabled. The outcome of the ensuing non-debatable voice vote to table was unclear so a division of the house was called. President Edens, who was presiding, called for those favoring to table to move to the right of the room and those opposed to move to the left. Such an obvious public vote made many faculty uncomfortable, especially young untenured faculty and undecided members who wished for further debate. The motion to table passed by 61 to 42 votes.

After adjournment internal debate continued. Some considered the issue resolved. Others wished to honor a distinguished alumnus and bring it up again. It became known that President Edens had asked Vice President Nixon to be com-

From the left, Duke President A. Hollis Edens, Vice President of the United States Richard M. Nixon, and classmate and later Duke trustee, Charles S. Rhyne.

mencement speaker and he had accepted. Proponents of the honorary degree, centered in the Law and Medical Schools, courted allies. Some thought it a duty to right the wrong of the previous faculty meeting and others did not wish to be manipulated by administrative maneuvering. The on campus debate became common knowledge when it was leaked to the press and appeared in the *New York Times* April 6. That story declared that Duke had denied a degree to Nixon and he had canceled his commencement talk. Public knowledge heightened campus debate.

The General Faculty next met on June 4. Two hundred and five were present, twice the number of the previous meeting. So many M.D.'s in white coats were in attendance that loud laughter ensued when someone shouted "Is there a doctor in the house?" Dean Joseph A. McClain of the Law School moved that the question of the Nixon degree be removed from the table. President Edens stated that the meeting was in executive session, as always, and if "anyone did not feel so bound he should withdraw." He further admonished that "This University has a right to expect a greater degree of integrity than was in evidence following the previous session." The Nixon honorary degree became an item of discussion by a vote of 111 to 86. It was then moved "to refer the whole problem of honorary degrees" to the University Council, an advisory governing body, "for study and appropriate action." The critical vote that that motion be tabled failed in a secret ballot by 93 to 105. Proponents of the Nixon honorary degree had won the right to a secret ballot but still could not muster a majority. An actual vote on whether or not to award Richard M. Nixon an honorary degree was then sidestepped by the vote to "refer and study the question of honorary degrees" which passed by 131 to 67.

On October 20, long after commencement, the University Council appointed a committee charging it to "take action on the specific item of a particular degree or to study the overall policy of awarding honorary degrees." On December 14, the committee presented a progress report saying further study was in order. A final committee report does not appear in the record. The University Council obviously had more pressing matters under deliberation. Its agenda was replete with studies and action regarding fringe benefits, desegregation, long range planning and its own organization since it was a relatively new experimental body. The University clearly had only deferred and not permanently tabled debate on alumnus, Richard M. Nixon. The question of an honorary degree had one further twist, however. The Associated Press reported in June, 1961, that Nixon had declined to accept an honorary degree offered from Duke that year.

The Duke Symposium Adds to Campus Intellectual Climate

The *Chronicle* called it "the most powerful educational jolt a student sponsored program has ever produced." The event was a three-day campus symposium in October, 1959 on "The U.S.-Soviet Conflict." The featured participants were Professors Merle Fainsod of Harvard University, Frederick Schuman of Williams College, and Thomas Whitney, a journalist with the Associated Press. The format was varied featuring formal addresses, panel discussions, classroom appearances, coffees, luncheons, dinners and receptions. The aim was "to make the campus come alive to the technological, social, and spiritual tensions between the two world powers." The impetus perhaps was Premier Nikita Khrushchev's assertion to the free world that "your grandchildren will live under Communism."

That initial Symposium under the direction of Senior Boyd Hight launched a successful annual series that ran for eleven years. In 1959, traditional campus programming consisted of a myriad of single events, but a few leaders remembered the popular annual series of Religious Emphasis Week from an earlier era. Following in that tradition they wished to pursue an intellectual topic in depth and present it to as many of the community as possible. With no budget and little time, Hight undertook the task in the late spring of 1959. A broad based committee was created to engage representatives of any established organization that might

The Duke Symposium usually ran for a week with topics of significance presented and discussed in a variety of ways across the campus.

contribute funds. Financial support came from such different sources as independent houses, living associations, fraternities, sororities, the YM and YWCA, student government associations and the Student Union. Later in 1965 the S and H Foundation awarded the Symposium a $1,500 grant as one of the thirty-eight most worthy, topical and significant public affairs programs in American universities.

The Symposium committee was self-perpetuating, consciously seeking committed, hard working participants from all four classes. Administrators and faculty joined out of interest and because of their expertise in certain subject areas. President Douglas M. Knight spoke or chaired a panel at several of the symposia. Cost was not prohibitive. It was the late 1960s before the committee made "the wrenching decision to pay over $1,000 for a speaker." Available reading lists and as many as twenty discussion groups sometimes preceded the main three-day event. Students sometimes visited Washington to interview prospective speakers with one delegation even going to the White House seeking the participation of President Eisenhower. The record reveals that many committee members and leaders are currently active faculty and alumni. One former chairman, Phil Lader, '66, has served President Clinton as Assistant to the President and Deputy Chief of Staff. He is perhaps more widely known, however, as the founder and convener of the ultimate symposium, the Renaissance Weekend which is held annually at Hilton Head resort every New Year's.

Student participation was a crucial part of the Symposium.

Throughout the decade, the year's symposium topics reflected the dominant concerns of the day—the Cold War and changing values. Topics were as varied as "Contemporary Literature and the Post-Christian Man," "Dimensions of Defense," "The Individual in Mass Society," and "Concepts of a University." In 1967 the students analyzed themselves in "Impact-the Post-War Generation" when they studied the "emerging generation that encompasses the Peace Corps, Black Power, marches, sit-ins and the battlefield."

By the late sixties, students questioned all institutions and they sometimes protested reflexively. The 1968 Symposium chaired by Peter English and titled "KAPOW, The Electric Media," was KO'd itself. On the second night, before an audience of a thousand people, eight students and a university employee stormed on stage and seized the microphones in Page Auditorium. They called for a "meaningful discussion to keep the Symposium from dying," and the panelists left the stage.

In the aftermath of the Silent Vigil, the university's largest protest to date, the previous spring, the Board of Trustees had enacted the school's first policy governing campus disruptions. The 1968 Symposium's protesters were the first students charged under the new Pickets and Protest policy. The dominant question quickly became the relevance of the new policy. The planning committee and the panel participants publicly noted that the disruption was more rude and abrupt than seriously disruptive. A required hearing was held. To the surprise of few on campus the students were acquitted of charges. Nevertheless, the divisive and disruptive incident affected the concept of a campus-wide symposium. In 1969 a Symposium half the size of previous ones was held on East Campus. A later brief attempt at revival failed to catch on.

For a decade, the Symposium lived up to its billing as the major educational event of the school year. It was more than just another extracurricular activity. It was, as publicized, "an ideal in action—students, faculty, administration, community coming together in responsible intellectual pursuit."

Divestment Drama: Trustees Listen to Student Protests

A "jail" was constructed on the Bryan Center walkway to symbolize the incarceration of those opposing apartheid in South Africa.

Commencement weekend in 1986 was one of the most tense and exhilarating in the history of Duke. The university community looked forward to Lee Iacocca's Sunday commencement speech with curiosity but it was the Saturday meeting of the Board of Trustees that aroused the most anticipation. The trustees' agenda called for a vote on the issue of the day on college campuses across the country—divestment or the sale of stock of corporations which operated in the Union of South Africa. Proponents of divestment believed the strategy would help topple the government that enforced the oppressive policy of apartheid. Under apartheid four and a half million whites had full rights of citizenship while twenty-one million blacks could not vote, buy or sell land, live or work where they chose, or move about freely. Duke had a modest portfolio of 188,300 shares of stock valued at $12,487,575 in 10 companies operating in South Africa, but the issue was more than economic. It involved political and social policy, but many believed it ultimately to be a moral issue.

The question of divestment had been building in the United States since the 1960s and it had been debated on campus since at least 1977 when the Radical Academic Union and the Black Student Alliance cooperated in forming the Duke South African Coalition. However, campus social action in the 1980s was quite different from the 1960s when the issue of Vietnam dominated everything. A small group of committed activists worked valiantly to bring concerns in South Africa to "mainstream middle class Dukies." They struggled with priorities, debated strategy, and attempted to build coalitions while facing the usual demands of papers and exams. When an informal poll in 1984 found that thirty percent of Duke students did not know what apartheid was and over fifty percent

did not understand divestment, simple education dictated strategy. The resulting educational campaign was quite successful. Within one year a student referendum narrowly favored divestment, and in two years significant pressure was brought on the Board of Trustees to support total divestment over a more cautious policy of selected divestment.

In a dramatic example of changing sentiment, worshipers on the way to a commencement weekend baccalaureate service in 1985 passed approximately seventy seniors in a silent vigil in front of the chapel protesting South African policy. The preacher, renowned activist William Sloan Coffin of Yale University, encouraged them in his sermon, and provided a meaningful, educational link with the earlier civil rights movement. Many of the protesting students surprised themselves by their actions. An organizer, Steve Rottman, had actually walked the beach signing up fellow seniors the previous week at the traditional final student fling at Myrtle Beach. Several protesters admitted to facing up to questions posed by their study abroad or in campus history, political science or public policy classes. Graduate student Mikel Taylor observed, encouraged, forced, and in time directed (if any one person could be characterized as director) the divestment campaign. Taylor, with a full beard and confrontational personality, both kept the campaign alive and alienated opponents and supporters with his 1960s-style hippie image.

The most dramatic event in the campaign was the appearance of Nobel Laureate, Bishop Desmond Tutu of South Africa in the Duke Chapel in January, 1986. Sponsored in part by the North Carolina Council of Churches, the rally raised public consciousness in the Triangle area and money for the anti-apartheid

Nobel Laureate, Bishop Desmond Tutu of South Africa spoke in Duke Chapel in 1986.

campaign in South Africa. Seeing and hearing Tutu in person energized students and united town and gown in the cause. Traditional tactics including a student led House Course and university sponsored symposia combined with innovative actions to educate the community. Taylor used the unlikely source of the popular personals section of the *Chronicle* to circulate such statements as "The leading cause of death among black children in South Africa is starvation. The leading cause of death among white children is drowning in a swimming pool."

Mobilizing student and public opinion was a necessity but ultimately university action depended upon the Board of Trustees. Newly inaugurated President H. Keith H. Brodie appointed new members to an established advisory body, the Committee on the Social Implications of Duke Investments. Chaired by Law professor Walter Dellinger, the committee consisted of four students, six faculty, two trustees and two administrators. With public awareness of the complex issue building, focus shifted to campus centers of authority. The committee's deliberations were crucial and gradually a position favoring conditional total divestment won over arguments for selective divestment. However, upon receipt of the report, the Trustees accepted only part of the report postponing final action pending further study and review of the position of the Academic Council. After a less than clear presentation and debate on the complex issues, the Academic Council voted 21 to 20 against the key provision calling for total divestment. Student activists had followed accepted channels of power working through committee deliberation, utilization of the position of young trustee, and student addresses to the Executive Committee and to the full Board, but with inconclusive results. Key student organizers began to believe they were "banging their head against a wall."

As the crucial trustee meeting during the 1986 commencement weekend approached, students went public with their campaign. A mock jail was built on the Bryan Center walkway to depict the lack of justice, and shanties illustrating the living conditions of most blacks in South Africa were erected in the main quad. The administration said students could occupy the shanties only during the day and that they had to be removed by the Board meeting and commencement weekend. Four seniors, two graduate students and one alumnus remained overnight, were arrested for trespassing, and taken to the Durham County jail. Duke's shantytown garnered national publicity along with similar structures on campuses across the country. The charges were dismissed when the students' lawyer pointed out that Duke students often slept overnight, outside on campus, especially before certain basketball games, without arrest for trespassing. He also stated that the administration was exporting its problems to the county court system. The removed shanties immediately went up again in anticipation of the weekend Board meeting and graduation festivities.

The Executive Committee of the Board deliberated three hours and recommended the more cautious approach of selective divestment. Student leaders Jan Nolting and John Humphrey, among others, again met individually and at a luncheon with trustees. Some trustees disliked pressure while one lamented "the loss of civility that ought to typify an academic institution." Trustees, faculty and students believed the moral stand for total divestment was lost, but some cautioned that minds were not yet made up. Mary Semans lobbied hard for total divestment at the annual trustee dinner which happened to be at her home Friday night. When the Board met Saturday morning the highly respected Sam Cook, who had been Duke's first black professor and was president of Dillard University, spoke forcefully in favor of a moral stand. Ambassador George McGhee, trustee emeritus, declared that he had been one who did not listen to students during Vietnam but that he had decided that they were right then, and now, and that they should not be ignored. Besides, he said, his granddaughter was graduating that weekend and she had urged him to speak in favor of total divestment. The tide began to turn and after lengthy, thorough and eloquent debate, the Board voted twenty-one to three for the more forceful strategy of total conditional divestment for the university. Chairman Neil Williams and President Brodie hastened to inform the awaiting students of the outcome. Most were very much surprised. As jubilant protesters tore down the shanties one student said, "We had a great protest planned for graduation but I'm happy to have to cancel it."

[This article is based on a 1988 history honors thesis," The Divestment Campaign at Duke University: Stepchild of the Civil Rights Movement" by Jana Eisinger.]

From the Beginning, University Employees Have Worked to Improve Durham _____

Duke University and Durham have had a long mutually supportive history. In the nineteenth century, the raw "boom town" needed a civilizing influence, and Trinity College wanted the bustling, presence of an urban "New South" city to attract faculty, students, and more certain financial support. The merger of town and gown in 1892 when Trinity College relocated to Durham has been quite successful. The first public meeting, the laying of the cornerstone for the main college building, was a festive occasion. A parade of bands, fire companies, city officials and all the schoolchildren marching by school set the mood. President John F. Crowell led a delegation of faculty and over fifty students from the college in Randolph County. After numerous speeches extolling the virtues of Durham and Trinity, the day concluded with the first football game witnessed in the city, a game between two Trinity club teams. It was evident that town and college personnel were overjoyed at the prospect of coming together.

Shortly after the school opened, however, a severe national economic depression seriously affected Trinity's financial status. Trinity survived for just the reasons Crowell stressed in relocating the school. An urban environment proved essential, and the mutual excitement over an unlimited future provided momentum. But, however welcome, the college provided much more than construction contracts, opportunity for employment, expanded market for town goods, and cultural and athletic entertainment. From the very beginning the city and the academic community depended on each other in tangible and intangible ways.

A conversation between Professor Edwin Mims of the English Department and members of the Canterbury Club, a local literary club, in June, 1895 began a process that resulted in the founding of a public library, the first tax supported public library in the state. The library also employed the first professional librarian and had the first bookmobile in the state. Numerous university personnel have assisted the public library, most notably University Librarian Benjamin E. Powell, who for nineteen years presided over the Library Advisory Board guiding the effort to secure funding for a desperately needed new building in 1980. The North Carolina Room in the Public Library is named in honor of Powell. The Durham County Public Library system, one of the most successful examples of town/gown interaction, is an example of an idea born in the formative time when the industrial city and the college community united to plan for a better life for all citizens.

One of the most visible examples of town/gown success is Southgate Dormitory on East Campus. James H. Southgate, popular Durham insurance man, was chairman of the Trinity board of trustees for twenty years. At his premature death in 1916, college administrators and townspeople sought to memorialize him with the construction of a dormitory. Townspeople exceeded their goal of $100,000 by $11,000, raising over one half of the building's total cost despite the difficult times of World War I. The memorial proved to be more than bricks and mortar. As the "most modern dormitory for women in the state," it had a major impact on the college. The enrollment of women doubled and the new facility provided dedicated space for greatly expanded programs for women. In one example, the town chapter of the American Association of University Women (AAUW) met in the dorm's auditorium providing interaction between the coeds and the college graduates of the city.

In January, 1928 the local newspaper proclaimed "the largest building permit in the history of Durham, if not in all the South, signed." Eventually $21,000,000 was expended in construction and furnishing of two new campuses for a new university. Such construction at the time of the stock market crash made Durham one of the few places with expanding employment opportunities. Jobs were available from stone setters and secretaries to professors and administrators. The opening of Duke University with its nine professional schools and colleges was a greater transformation of an institution in a shorter period of time than had ever occurred in the history of higher education in the South.

The presence of a university had a dramatic impact on the city. Campus expertise reinforced town initiatives for improvement and led in new directions as well. For example, in 1934 the AAUW request for a much needed new separate Juvenile Court won approval with support from a study commission chaired by Professor John Bradway of the Duke Law School. Bradway was a nationally respected legal scholar who also established an innovative local legal aid society that benefited both the town and law school. In education and child care, kindergartens operated by Duke departments of psychology and education reinforced efforts providing nursery schools and medical care for Durham's low income families. The new Durham Nursery School Association also helped upgrade standards.

Sociology professor, Howard E. Jensen, is representative of many who worked quietly in public service never expecting to receive acclaim. Jensen helped start the United Way and State Commission for the Blind. Professor Louise Hall worked tirelessly in support of campus custodian, J. L. Alexander, who operated Walltown Charitable Community Center in the neighborhood north of East Campus. Professor Orrin Pilkey often took Walltown children on trips to the

University Librarian Benjamin E. Powell (1905–1981) is one of many Duke faculty and staff who have contributed time and talent to Durham city and county affairs.

Duke Marine Lab for their first visit to the ocean.

In addition to the obvious asset of the Duke Hospital and Medical School, additional developments such as the founding of the Hospital for Crippled Children, now the Lenox Baker Children's Hospital, and the Hospital Care Association, now Blue Cross/Blue Shield, benefited all citizens alike. Too numerous to mention, similar programs have emanated from the Divinity, Nursing, Graduate and Business Schools, and the School of the Environment, each contributing to a better life in Durham. In 1997 a Community Service Center coordinates myriad undergraduate volunteer efforts and a Durham Neighborhood Initiative offers a more focused university endeavor in the city.

In the 1990s, a "what-have-you-done-for-me-lately" mentality often obscures the all important historical perspective. Unfortunately, it is not uncommon to hear allusions to "university indifference to community affairs" and read preposterous statements like "the Gothic architecture on West Campus was an intentional effort [by Duke] to distance itself from the community." After a century it is clear town/gown relations have progressed at an uneven pace but they have been quite active and remarkably positive, primarily because the city and university have gown and matured together. The nineteenth century town known as a crude but suitable place to start a business has evolved into a sophisticated urban area with a wide range of assets. The struggling college of 1892 has established its identity as a major university with a unique mix of schools emphasizing teaching and research. Through the decades, both town and gown have assisted and learned from each other for the mutual benefit of all.

A Duke student helping young girls learn to sew at Walltown Charitable Community Center near East Campus.

Qualifications for a University President: James R. Killian's Report Timeless

The most important decision made by a Board of Trustees is the selection of a president. That decision has been made twelve times in the history of the institution and six times under the name of Duke University. Each presidential search is unique, but one historical document from the search in 1948 is not without relevance because of its cogent definition of the office of president. In 1948, Duke University had changed leadership only once when Vice President Robert L. Flowers became president in 1940 at the unexpected death of President William P. Few. There had been only one other change at the top in the twentieth century when Dean Few succeeded John C. Kilgo as President of Trinity College in 1910. With so little recent institutional history in choosing a president, Willis Smith, Chairman of the Board of Trustees, understandably sought advice as he directed the process in 1948.

James R. Killian, Jr., a native South Carolinian and former student at Trinity College, was Vice President of Massachusetts Institute of Technology. For all practical purposes, Killian was running MIT since its president, Karl Compton, was heavily involved in governmental scientific work. Undoubtedly, Smith had

The Chapel Court above the Main Quadrangle has been the favored location for presidential inaugurations.

Killian in mind as a possible candidate for the Duke vacancy. To initiate contact, Smith asked Killian to outline the most desired qualifications for a university president. Killian's response, a three-page "job description" dated July 30, demonstrates profound understanding of a complex and often misunderstood position.

First of all, Killian emphasized, the ideal university president should possess demonstrated administrative ability. In practice that meant "coordinating students, staff, trustees, and alumni in a common enthusiasm and working with the faculty as a company of scholars rather than managing them through a line organization." Second, the president should have a keen sense of public relations and the capacity to express the aims and ideals of the university while becoming, as a third requirement, a symbol of the standards and ideals of the university. Fourth, the president should be "courageous in maintaining high standards" because "the strength of a great university depends upon the quality of its graduates." Fifth, the ideal leader understands the partnership between research and teaching with each strengthening the other. This partnership must be carefully nurtured in the university setting between graduate, professional and undergraduate faculty. But Killian noted, "students and staff must have a sense of community responsibility, a sense of belonging" in the partnership of research and teaching as well.

Sixth, Killian believed an active interest in public service was essential because the willingness to render service to the community, state, and nation and to inspire others to do so was a vitalizing quality. Seventh, the president should be able to handle financial affairs in a manner both to conserve and to enlarge resources. To that end, calculated risks were permissible if one remembered that funds must be kept at work in the most productive fashion. Eighth, the president should have strength and stamina along with a proper outlook. In the final analysis, he believed an extrovert was more likely to succeed than one too introspective. For the ninth qualification, the proper university leader should possess interest in people and enthusiasm for helping them.

Cognizant of the unique role of privately endowed institutions, Killian added four qualifications pertinent to schools such as Duke. First, the successful president must realize that the independence and flexibility of private universities enabled them to be pace setters and set standards if they were organized to move quickly and take advantage of special situations. Second, the wise leader recognized that the regional characteristics of a university were a source of strength and individuality, for to function properly a private university had to be a vital part of the community in which it lived. Third, the president should maintain contacts with national professional and scholarly societies to keep in touch with new ideas and the best minds in the country. Finally, to Killian one of the central problems in contemporary education, "that of combining an education designed to help one earn a living with an education to help one become a well-rounded person," demanded strong institutional leadership. His ideal university president should recognize "that utility in education is not enough, that training for citizenship and spiritual values must have a central place in any great university."

Smith and other Duke personnel were greatly impressed with Killian and after visits to Durham he and his wife were excited by the opportunity at Duke. However, further contact abruptly ceased with a telegram dated September 17 saying "unexpected and compelling developments" made it wise to remain at MIT. Killian had met with the Executive Committee of his Board of Trustees the previous day. Their deliberations became common knowledge two weeks later when he was named president of MIT. He remained a friend of Duke receiving an honorary degree in 1949, speaking at Founders' Day in 1950, and serving as one of the leaders in the Capital Campaign of 1965. Another legacy is Killian's astute observations on the role of a university president.

Presidential Searches Have a Varied History___

In December, 1992, Nannerl O. Keohane was elected by the Board of Trustees to serve as the eighth president of Duke University and the thirteenth president of the institution. The following was shared with the university community as historical background in understanding the selection process. It was written prior to the announcement that the new president would be the first woman to hold that position in the history of the institution.

The eight twentieth-century presidents who have served Trinity College and Duke University form an interesting profile. All male, none have been alumni of Duke University. Serving an average of 13 years as president, their tenure has ranged from the 30-year term of William P. Few (1910–1940) to the 3-year tenure of J. Deryl Hart (1960–1963). Six presidents have been Southerners with two each being natives of North Carolina, South Carolina and Georgia while one has been a native of Massachusetts and one of Connecticut. Five have been Methodists. By training one was a preacher (John C. Kilgo), one a graduate of the U. S. Naval Academy (Robert L. Flowers), two have earned Ph.D. degrees in English (William P. Few from Harvard and Douglas M. Knight from Yale), one

New symbols of office, a mace and chain, were first used at the inauguration of President Terry Sanford. Processing here are J. H. Phillips, University Marshal, William S. Hecksher (partially hidden) carrying the mace, and President Sanford wearing the chain of office.

earned a Ph.D. degree in Public Administration (A. Hollis Edens from Harvard), one was a lawyer (Terry Sanford, University of North Carolina) and two were doctors (J. Deryl Hart, Johns Hopkins and H. Keith H. Brodie, Columbia).

Four presidents have been selected from outside the university community and four have been elevated from within. Their average age upon selection has been 51 ranging from 33 for John C. Kilgo to 71 for Robert L. Flowers. Internal candidates who became president averaged 57 years of age while those selected from outside the university averaged 44 years.

Almost as important in the academic community as who was selected president has been the process of selection itself. While arguably the most significant responsibility of the board of trustees, the selection of a president has evolved to include the total university community, especially the faculty.

The first change of leadership of the modern institution came in 1894 at the crucial time of financial stringency and acclamation to the new urban location. A committee of trustees composed of three representatives from each of the two constituent North Carolina conferences of the Methodist Church made the selection. When lobbying began for favorite candidates, benefactor Benjamin N. Duke clearly stated, "I do not care to enter into the contest. I do not propose to let such matters bother and harass me." When the committee's first choice turned them down, it recommended a popular young minister who was the financial agent of Wofford College, John C. Kilgo, to the board of trustees. Kilgo's selection proved fortuitous since he served for sixteen successful years before becoming a bishop in the Methodist Church.

Few records exist for the selection of Kilgo's successor but undoubtedly little discussion was necessary. Kilgo's choice, William P. Few, who was then Professor of English and the first Dean of the College, became president in 1910. The students approval was evident in the *Chronicle's* comment that continued rapid strides were expected under Few's leadership and that "it will not be many more years until Trinity College will be really and truly the 'Harvard of the South'." Few modestly wrote Ben Duke, "I am very glad to have a place where, under fortunate circumstances, I can engage in useful work." His thirty year tenure which included the first fifteen years of Duke University proved the most significant in the history of the school.

Few's death on October 16, 1940 marked the only time a Duke president has died in office. As senior vice president of business affairs, Robert L. Flowers was named acting president. Within four months his fifty years of service as teacher and administrator was recognized with his official elevation to the presidency. Flowers had been professor of mathematics, secretary and treasurer of the university, and successor to James B. Duke on the board of the Duke Endowment. Upon his resignation in 1948 he accepted the then honorary position of chancellor.

At the passing of a half century of stable leadership and in the face of numerous pressing post-World War II problems, the faculty sought greater influence in the governing of the university. The chairman of the board, Willis Smith, agreed to faculty participation in the selection of Flowers' successor if it were clearly understood that it was consultative only. Smith suggested that all department chairmen and deans meet and select a faculty committee with at least one woman member to consult with the trustee committee. A faculty committee of five was selected, chaired by Newman I. White of the English department with Katherine Gilbert of philosophy as the female representative. The committee was asked for a profile of an ideal president plus its preference for either an internal or external candidate.

In November, 1948, Smith excited the campus with the announcement of the selection of A. Hollis Edens as president. Edens, age 47, was a native of Tennessee who had risen meteorically in the Georgia state system of higher education before becoming an officer in the Rockefeller Foundation.

After Hollis Edens resigned in 1960 the selection process became refined as J. Deryl Hart, chairman of the department of surgery, became president pro-tem and then president. On at least one occasion resumes of presidential candidates were read and discussed in a called meeting of trustees, administrators and faculty. Many resolutions and meetings of trustee-faculty liaison committees helped balance desired and legally defined responsibilities.

The trustees and faculty worked well together in the selection of Douglas M. Knight as president in 1963. Knight, a specialist in nineteenth century English literature, was president of Lawrence College in Appleton, Wisconsin. Succeeding Nathan Pusey who left Lawrence to head Harvard University, Knight was one of an impressive list of presidents who went on to universities giving Lawrence College the appellation "training ground of presidents."

At the time of the selection of Knight's successor in 1969, chairman of the board, Charles B. Wade, named the prototype of the current selection committee. Consisting of seventeen members Wade's committee had nine trustees, five faculty with five alternates, one alumni representative and two students. John C. McKinney, vice provost and dean of the graduate school chaired the search committee. He was assisted by a three-person administrative staff. The committee drew up a profile of twelve criteria for president articulating for the first time the permissibility of "the functional equivalent of a broad university background and an earned doctorate." The creation of the office of chancellor in addition to that of provost permitted serious consideration of individuals with traditionally non-academic backgrounds. The committee took just such a path in recommending the election of Terry Sanford, a lawyer, politician and popular former governor of North Carolina as president.

The search committees in 1984 and 1992 have been identical in representative composition. They were made up of six trustees, six faculty, two alumni, an undergraduate and a graduate student, a university staff employee, and a representative from the Durham community. The 1984 committee, chaired by trustee John Forlines with faculty representative, Bob Durden, as vice chairman, recommended that H. Keith H. Brodie, chancellor and former chairman of the department of psychiatry, be elected president. The current search committee is chaired by trustee John W. Chandler with Philip Stewart of the faculty as vice chairman.

Currently, the long-sought faculty participation in the selection of a president is recognized through representation on the search committee. The academic council nominates a number of faculty representatives from which the board of trustees selects members for the search committee. The chairman of the academic council serves ex officio on the committee as well. Individual faculty are solicited for nominations for president. Deliberations of the search committee itself are conducted in utmost secrecy. Recent broadening of representation in the process of selecting a president has coincided with the increasingly secretive deliberations of the duly constituted search committee. The ultimate authority in the selection of a president remains, as always, with the full membership of the board of trustees.

Men and Women In Blue: Campus Police Began With Four Officers _____

One of the most dramatic and significant changes at Duke through the years has been the evolution of a campus police force. The exact origin of a campus as opposed to a city police presence is impossible to determine but typically campus police duties arose from an extension of service responsibilities such as maintaining heat and electric power for the college community. Night duty personnel added the responsibility of checking buildings and grounds for safety, often becoming deputized by a government authority if necessary. Campus police probably originated at Trinity College in the 1920's as the original physical facilities were being redesigned and rebuilt and vastly expanded with the construction of an added campus to the west.

When Bennett Jackson retired in 1970 after thirty-one years of service he reported joining a force of four in 1939. When he began everyone worked two shifts—sunup to sundown and sundown to sunup. According to Jackson all that was needed most often to control students was "to bluff 'em. Just mention the dean's name. That was enough." The primary duty of traffic control consisted of overseeing only about 300 cars on campus.

When Merle O. Crittenton joined the force in 1961, he was given a uniform, a weapon, and a beat. The force of less than ten had one car. When backup transportation was necessary they had access to a campus plumbing truck. Crittenton notes that by far the greatest change he has experienced is in training. When he was employed it was assumed that men knew how to handle a gun and he was given no weapon's training. Today officers undertake sixteen weeks of training before a weapon is issued and training is on-going.

Currently, professionalism and visibility characterize the department. Change began under the leadership of Chiefs W. C. A. Bear in 1961 and C. J. Vizas in 1969 but it dramatically accelerated with the arrival of Paul J. Dumas in 1971. In 1965, a North Carolina law gave campus police the option to cease being special deputies and became full fledged police with the power to arrest and carry arms. Duke exercised that option immediately. The small program which was run out of basement offices on West Campus, first in 001 Divinity and then in 012 Social Science, expanded into larger quarters at 2010 Campus Drive. On Paul Dumas's first day, December 6, 1971, the name of the program was changed from Traffic and Security to Public Safety and its reporting relationship was moved from Physical Plant Operations to Business Administration. The program also was divided into Police Operations and Safety and Traffic Divisions. A detective unit was begun in 1972. Administrators clearly decided to create a true professional force for the university instead of relying so much on off-duty city police to assist on campus. As a further example of professionalism in the campus force, state law began requiring psychological testing of prospective police officers on January 1, 1995. The first documented example of such testing at Duke is 1959.

Changes in undergraduate life greatly influenced campus safety. Increases in the numbers of students, faculty and staff as well as expansion of the campus brought dramatic changes in the prevalence of automobiles with consequent concerns for traffic control and parking. Increasing student activism challenged authority making the college campus the center of protests for change. Outsiders came on campus in increasing numbers transforming what had been traditionally a relatively peaceful setting into often an area of conflict. Changes in habits of dress made it more difficult to identify visitors and intruders from members of the university community. At Duke the merging of the Woman's College with Trinity College ended the separation of men and women on different campuses thus further complicating provisions for safety. Such societal changes along with the traditional tension inherent with youth becoming independent adults makes the college campus of the 1990s vastly different from the 1920s.

A college campus, especially a research university with a vast medical complex, is akin to a small city in many respects. In 1994 the Duke police division alone ranked twenty-fifth in size in the state of North Carolina. If the fifty-nine security officers were added to the sixty-nine police officers the division would rank even higher. The division also owned fifteen vehicles.

The university community relies heavily on the public safety department often taking its presence for granted. Their advance planning and performance of duty make possible the appearance of distinguished visitors like Prime Minister Pierre Trudeau of Canada, Archbishop and Nobel Prize winner Desmond Tutu of South Africa or former President Jimmy Carter. Police and security officers have risked their lives to successfully evacuate sleeping students from burning dormitories. A prolonged

Duke Public Safety inaugurates a bicycle patrol.

hostage situation in the Medical Center probably represents the most serious incident to occur on campus.

Not content to react to events, the heart of the public safety philosophy is education. Yet it is a constant challenge to get the community, especially students, to assume more responsibility for individual and collective safety. The Duke Department of Public Safety is well positioned to assist and cover the campus. Early telephone book listings cited numbers to call for help on campus but they gave no locations to seek assistance! Today's telephone listing reflects the availability and vast change in campus protection and security. In addition to a physical, post office and FAX address, names and numbers are given for department administrators, police offices on campus and in the medical center, and for divisions and programs in security, traffic enforcement, special events, human relations, safe-walk/safe rides and victim assistance. One doubts if police work on campus were really as simple as it seemed years ago. However, there is no doubt that it has evolved into a complex undertaking. Duke benefits greatly from having a truly professional public safety department.

The Tradition of Graduation Distinguishes Duke's Most Significant Convocation

Commencement weekend, with its formal Baccalaureate services and graduation ceremony, follows traditions as ancient and universal as those from the first

A student marshal.

medieval universities, and as unique as the evolutionary practices of Duke University. Graduation is our most significant convocation where undergraduate and graduate students, faculty, alumni, friends, and distinguished guests gather in celebration and to honor the purpose of the institution. The graduation ceremony is significant as part of Duke's long standing history as well as because it is part of an ancient tradition. The diploma, academic regalia with distinctive identifying colors and symbols, and the mace and chain of office are traditions centuries old.

At Duke, many commencement weekend traditions date from the early decades of the origin of the university in 1838 as Union Institute. Current traditions firmly established by the name change to Trinity College in 1859 include the recognition of graduation with distinction, the noting of special honors and prizes, the awarding of honorary degrees, the selection of student speakers, the distribution of Bibles to undergraduates, and the hosting of a gala outdoor reception in honor of graduates and their families. One confusing item might be that, for example, Commencement, 1990, represents the 138th official exercise. This particular accounting derives from the fact that in 1852 the legislature of North Carolina officially granted the institution authority to award degrees. At that date, the academy became a college.

While full of tradition in one sense, commencement observances reflect changing times as well. In the 19th century, the exercises sometimes lasted a week. Today official ceremonies occur over Friday, Saturday, and Sunday only. Through the years in Durham, the location of graduation has changed from Epworth Inn and Craven Memorial Hall on the Trinity College campus to Page Auditorium, the Chapel, Cameron Indoor Stadium, the main quadrangle of East Campus, and Wallace Wade Stadium on the Duke University campus. During World War II, degrees were awarded in official ceremonies, complete with a speaker, as often as six times a year.

Innovation is evident as well in the scheduling of multiple Baccalaureate services. Since 1975, students have requested three identical services in order to accommodate the number of students and parents wishing to participate in this impressive ceremony in Duke Chapel.

Two modern adaptations of ancient practices concern the nature of the diploma itself and the wearing of an official Duke academic robe. Today's diplomas are no longer literally sheepskin. Quality paper of high rag content is far more long lasting than animal skin or vellum, which wrinkles considerably thus distorting the text. Since 1969, a registered dye of official Duke blue has been used for the doctoral robes of the university. This distinctive robe with its soft black tam instead of a mortarboard instantly identifies the wearer as a recipient of Duke's most prestigious degree.

Through the years, important milestones have been part of commencement activities. In the 19th century, the first earned M.A. degrees were awarded in 1877; and Mary, Persis, and Theresa Giles became the first women graduates with B.A. degrees in 1878. The first Ph.D. degrees were awarded in 1928 to Frederick Holl and Dean Rumbold in Zoology. Campus events as part of commencement activities have included the unveiling of the statues of Washington Duke in 1908 and James B. Duke in 1935, and the laying of the cornerstone of Southgate dormitory in 1921 and Alumni Memorial Gym in 1922. As a teenager Doris Duke, the only daughter of James B. Duke, assisted in the laying of the cornerstone of West Campus in 1928. The inaugural carillon and organ recitals were part of the festivities when the Chapel was used for the first time at commencement in 1932.

Despite the pomp and pageantry and historical milestones, the conferring of degrees, both earned and honorary, represent the high point of any ceremony. The university usually confers over twenty different degrees upon approximately 2,800 graduates. With four different names, two major locations and expanding curricula and sites, historical references for Duke University can be confusing. However, the honoring of students upon completion of a prescribed program of studies has been part of each academic year in the history of the institution.

Holiday Traditions of Duke

One sometimes encounters the sentiment that Duke University is too young to have traditions. If a tradition is literally the passing of cultural behavior from generation to generation, maybe we observe as many "time-honored practices" at the Christmas holiday season as traditions. However, one annual campus event has become a true tradition. George Frederic Handel's oratorio, the *Messiah*, was first performed in Duke Chapel on December 10, 1933, in only the second year that the Chapel was in use. Curiously, it took time for university officials to become accustomed to the Gothic architecture of the impressive new building. After one Christmas celebration utilizing the Men's and Women's Glee Clubs, J. Foster Barnes, the Director of Choral Music, decided that having the Chapel Choir perform selections from Handel's *Messiah* might be more appropriate to the setting. The program became an instant success and to many today the performance marks the beginning of the Christmas season, even more so than putting up the tree or beginning the holiday round of parties.

In a letter to the *Chronicle*, an alumnus of the law school recounted his recollections of one memorable performance of the *Messiah*. He and his date left the Chapel after the stirring "Hallelujah Chorus" only to discover a hushed and fearful

The annual performance of Handel's oratorio, the Messiah, *by the chapel choir has been a Duke tradition since 1933.*

campus as news of the bombing of Pearl Harbor spread that Sunday afternoon, December 7, 1941. He further reported that the next time he heard the "Hallelujah Chorus" it was on Armed Forces Radio after the announcement of the end of the war in the Pacific theater. To him the "Hallelujah Chorus" marked the beginning and end of World War II.

When the demand exceeded capacity for the *Messiah* a second Christmas program patterned after the service of Lessons and Carols at King's College, Cambridge, was begun. This Christmas Eve service was begun in 1969 by James T. Cleland, Dean of the Chapel; J. Benjamin Smith, Director of Chapel Music; and Dr. James G. Ferguson, Jr., friend of the Chapel. This service consciously unites town and gown with participants from the university community, an invited local guest choir, and a volunteer Duke and community choir. Since this 11:00 p.m. service now exceeds capacity of the Chapel, an afternoon children's service and a 5:30 p.m. family service have been added.

A more student-oriented and campus-centered program which is on the way to becoming a tradition is the Duke Holiday Tree Lighting Ceremony sponsored by the University Union. Begun in 1972, it is now an annual observance. This ecumenical service brightens the campus as the semester draws to a close at exam time. The Carillon and Duke Chorale provide music, the food service has refreshments, and the President of the University lights the campus tree. Surprisingly, the celebration almost ended in controversy in its second year. President Richard M. Nixon, in "Operation Independence," appealed to the nation in December, 1973, to conserve energy in the first national energy crisis. Part of his program included the elimination of Christmas lighting to conserve energy. That request was hotly debated by the student legislature and rejected when a proposal for a "non-lighting tree ceremony" was overwhelming rejected. The university cut the number of bulbs by half and lit the tree only five hours per day but nevertheless there was considerable adverse publicity. Many students wanted a brightly lit tree because of the academic pressures they faced and President Terry Sanford noted that the University was cutting back thermostats and reducing lighting as a contribution to the energy crisis. Calling Nixon's appeal to dim Christmas lights "ninety-nine percent show," Sanford said, "We need to light up our spirits." The Associated Press reported nationwide that "the energy crisis has collided with the spirit of Christmas at Duke University and that Christ-

J. Foster Barnes (1894–1956), Director of Choral Music from 1927 to 1956 initiated many traditions enjoyed today.

mas has won." Student planners proceeded nervously but they were rewarded when one thousand participants showed up for the campus ceremony, all in enthusiastic support of lighting the tree. The ceremony also has had its humorous moments. In 1978 Santa Claus planned a dramatic appearance by rappelling down the face of the Union tower. However, his beard became entangled in the ropes and he became suspended without any rescuing reindeer in sight.

The holiday spirit is evident in the main quadrangle during the day with the display of oversized green wreaths with big red bows by the entrance to the Chapel. This decoration is much appreciated by members of the campus community who do not see the tree lit at night. These wreaths plus the Advent Wreath and special decorations in the Chapel are provided by the Elizabeth Lucina Gotham Memorial Endowment established by Dr. and Mrs. James H. Semans. This fund is a memorial to Miss Elizabeth Gotham (1887–1968), a very close friend who was employed by Mary Duke Biddle and Mary D. B. T. Semans for forty-six years.

Campus holiday observances have not always been so festive. In the nineteenth century it was not uncommon for students to remain at school without a break and President Braxton Craven believed that Christmas should best be celebrated with solemnity. A student wrote his parents in 1879 that he had "never witnessed such a dull Christmas before."

Campus observances have varied greatly through the years and some significant practices have ceased with changing times. For years the women students in Brown House on East Campus had the popular Dean of the Chapel, James T. Cleland, who was a native of Scotland, appear at their annual Christmas party as Mr. McClaus. While Cleland's seasonal readings in his Scottish brogue no longer continue, his name is prominently displayed in the main quadrangle of West Campus. As the first women's dorm to transfer to West Campus, Brown House could not transfer its name as well. Out of gratitude to Cleland's special relationship to their dorm, the women of Brown House adopted the name Cleland when they moved to West.

Traditions are significant in the life of any institution and Duke's holiday traditions are especially welcome as the semester comes to an end and the exam period looms.

The University and the Cigar:
A Century-Old Link with Tobacco _____

Duke's Mixture was a popular tobacco product of the American Tobacco Company around 1900.

Tobacco always has been controversial. Shortly after Sir Walter Raleigh transported tobacco from the recently discovered colonies to England, King James I published a "Counterblaste to Tobacco." Writing in 1604, he called smoking "a custom loathsome to the eye, hateful to the nose, harmful to the brain, and dangerous to the lungs." To this day proponents and opponents of the "golden weed" have argued their case and many have been drawn into the debate whether directly or indirectly. As one would expect, neither Trinity College nor Duke University has escaped the maelstrom.

Trinity College became forever associated with tobacco in 1892 when it relocated to Durham, a city built on the manufacture of tobacco and its associated products. At that time Durham was producing more cigarettes than any place on earth and the primary benefactors of the college were the Dukes, a family that had emerged as the predominant entrepreneurs in the cutthroat competition in the industry due to the business genius of James B. Duke.

The Dukes were wealthy and founders of the tobacco trust amidst a poor, agriculturally based economy. They were unabashedly Republican in a predominately Democratic state with a growing anti-establishment Populist Party. They were also sympathetic to African Americans when race baiting was the norm in political, economic and social relations. In addition to all of the above, several subplots enlivened the mix of college public relations. Moralists were anti-tobacco, especially toward the new form of cigarettes. North Carolina Methodists were divided for the first time into two administrative conferences and upon relocation Trinity moved from one area to another leaving a small but vocal residue of ill will. John C. Kilgo, the new Trinity president in 1894, wisely embraced the Dukes as the best means for consistent financial support for the college. Moreover, Kilgo, a spellbinding orator destined to be elected a Methodist Bishop, had supreme confidence in his own ability and he did not back down in a fight. He added to the fray by leading private denominational colleges in extolling the advantages of Christian education over secular education, and he even participated in a secret legislative agreement to limit financial support for the University of North Carolina.

Hence, Trinity, tobacco, Duke and Kilgo were rarely out of the news. One libel suit against Kilgo was heard before the state supreme court three times before he won acquittal. Only once did the Kilgo-Duke partnership bend to public criticism. Washington Duke gave three, $100,000 gifts of tobacco company stock for college endowment. At his second donation in 1898, he was persuaded to switch the gift from tobacco stock to the Virginia-Carolina Chemical Company. The college paid dearly as that stock's dividends proved to be uncertain and it declined in value.

The Dukes learned to live with criticism. James B. Duke ignored it. As creator of the American Tobacco Company, the Southern (now Duke) Power Company and the family philanthropic foundation, The Duke Endowment, he accentuated the positive claiming his greatest accomplishment was in "making men."

He prided himself in building industries that provided large scale employment, and in identifying potential for leadership and rewarding successful associates. The college and later university administration also put up with taunts that the school's motto was Eruditio et Religio et Cigaretto. Some wags even claimed to have heard administrators say in frustration "Sure the money is tainted. Taint yours."

When the statue of James B. Duke was unveiled in the main quadrangle on West Campus at commencement in 1935, even that occasion proved to be controversial. No one questioned the appropriateness or the right to recognize the institution's primary benefactor with a larger than life bronze statue, but the cigar in his hand set off debate. Students circulated a petition opposing the statue or at least requesting that it be located in an adjacent quadrangle. Opponents feared that "the cigar would attract more attention than the chapel itself" and that "Duke University will be known as a gift from which the price tag has never been removed." President Few silenced the opposition noting that carefully drawn and approved plans always had planned to memorialize Duke in the main quadrangle and that he "would gladly honor him in any way, however conspicuous, for the power of his example as a great benefactor and lover of mankind."

It was perhaps surprising that students would protest Duke's cigar because smoking was becoming part of campus culture. However, women smoking, even in the tobacco state of North Carolina posed a dilemma. The Woman's College

Surprisingly Duke students objected to the cigar in James Duke's hand when his statue was unveiled in the main quad in 1935.

student government association debated the issue and arrived at a compromise permitting women students to smoke in their own rooms, dormitory parlors and private homes but not elsewhere on campus or in public in Durham. Town-gown interests merged humorously in the 1930s in one cheer at athletic contests: Chesterfield, Bull Durham, [Lucky] Strikes and Plug, Duke University Slug, Slug, Slug.

Ironically, today the "town renowned around the world" for tobacco takes pride in being called the "City of Medicine." At Duke, non-smoking areas have been creeping across campus until vast areas are smoke free. The Medical Center first banned smoking in its buildings in 1989 and Perkins Library and Cameron Indoor Stadium followed suit. The Provost issued a memorandum banning smoking in all classrooms in 1991. Employee services even include access to smoking cessation seminars. Sponsored research has run the gamut from grants from tobacco companies early in the century to support for documenting the harmful effects of tobacco today. Clearly despite its location and basis of financial support, Duke University has never been far from controversy in the continuous debate over the use of tobacco.

Letterhead of stationery from W. Duke Sons & Co.

Outdoor Statues Connect Present to Past

Visible symbols of history and traditions are important for institutions like a university where there is a constant graduation of a large portion of the community. At Duke, staff, students, alumni and visitors are reminded of benefactors and the contributions of significant personnel from portraits, statuary, memorial plaques and the naming of campus sites. Duke University is fortunate to have exceptional examples of outdoor statuary to honor those who have made worthy contribution to its history.

Washington Duke, who began the family's tie to Trinity College with a donation of money for buildings and endowment in 1890, is memorialized by a unique seated statue on East Campus. After Duke's death in 1905 a spontaneous movement developed among friends to honor him. Organizers from Richmond, Virginia signed a curiously worded contract for "a seated bronze statue, size as if standing 7 feet" with native sculptor Edward Virginius Valentine. Known as "the South's greatest sculptor," Valentine then sixty-seven years old, had studied abroad in Paris, Florence and Berlin. He returned home to Richmond in 1865 to launch a career memorializing famous southerners. Even in an impoverished region, he had commissions from as far as Lexington, Kentucky (Vice-President John C. Breckinridge), New Orleans (John James Audubon) and Richmond (Thomas Jefferson as well as many Confederate heroes). His most famous statue is the recumbent Robert E. Lee in Lee's Chapel, Washington and Lee University. Valentine's studio is part of the respected Valentine Museum in downtown Richmond.

Edward Valentine's unusual seated statue of benefactor Washington Duke was unveiled in 1908.

On West Campus, James B. Duke, son of Washington Duke and creator of the Duke Endowment and founder of Duke University, is memorialized larger than life by Charles Keck. Keck, son of German immigrants, was born in New York City where he studied at the National Academy of Design before continuing his education in Greece, Italy and France. He was assistant to Augustus St. Gaudens from 1893 to 1898. Keck's work is described as being in the classic tradition of Gaudens but one critic noted that Keck often added "his own touch through nervous movement and veristic details." His inclusion of the characteristic cigar and the slight movement evident in the use of a cane in Duke's statue appear to be such signature touches. Keck also carved the three Duke marble sarcophagi in the Memorial Chapel and the nearby bronze statue of the three Presidents of the United States from North Carolina in the Capitol Square in Raleigh. Keck's work is exhibited in at least sixteen states and two foreign countries. Perhaps the most visible of his works are a statue of Father Duffy in Times Square and the heroic female figure at the entrance to Columbia University in New York City. Additional well known and unique statues of his include Booker T. Washington in Tuskegee, Alabama and a young Abraham Lincoln in Wabash, Indiana. Keck's son, Charles, earned A.B. and M.D. degrees from Duke in 1949 and 1953.

The sculptor most frequently represented on campus is an alumnus, Franklin Creech, A.B. 1964. Creech attended Duke on a football scholarship, earning his varsity letter on ACC championship teams. After an art major at Duke, Creech earned a masters degree at Florida State University. Through the years he has taught in public schools, community colleges and colleges and universities, including Duke, in North Carolina. Since 1977 he has operated a complete foundry workshop in his hometown of Smithfield, NC that houses welding, woodworking, stained glass, pottery, drawing and painting studios.

Creech's contributions to his alma mater are numerous. The department of athletics first commissioned him to make a bronze bust of Wallace Wade. The likeness was so successful and admired that additional commissions followed with mounted busts of William D. "Bill" Murray, Edmund M. "Eddie" Cameron, and John Wesley "Jack" Coombs now marking athletic facilities named in their honor. Creech also produces a 10 inch replica of the statue of the Sower on East Campus for the university's office of development. This replica is the symbol of the Founders' Society which recognizes major donors to university endowments. Over eight hundred of the personally crafted replicas have been presented to significant donors. Creech also has crafted a bronze Blue Devil that the president of the university presents in recognition of extraordinary volunteer service to Duke. It is gratifying that the popular sculptures in the athletic sector of the campus and the much appreciated symbols of gratitude for a vital continuing relationship to the university are the product of an alumnus.

The most recent addition of sculpture to the campus is the most unusual. A life-size camel and man, cast in bronze, called "Nature and the Scientist," honoring James B. Duke Professor Emeritus Knut Schmidt-Nielsen was unveiled in 1996. Schmidt-Nielsen, a native of Norway, joined the Duke Zoology Department in 1952. His primary research on how animals survive in harsh climates included renowned studies of the camel. The dramatic sculpture was designed and executed by the English artist and zoologist Jonathan Kingdon. It is the first outdoor sculpture to honor a member of the faculty.

Frank Creech's statue of John Wesley "Jack" Coombs (1882–1957), baseball great and longtime Duke coach, identifies Coombs Field in the West Campus athletic complex.

The Student Education Initiative:
_____ Separating the Myths From Duke's History

Here at Duke myths prevail. One constantly hears the fictional account of James B. Duke offering his fortune to Princeton if only it would change its name to Duke and, failing in that endeavor, then finding Trinity College in Durham which agreed to his terms. Confusion about our history abounds. We have had four, or is that five, name changes and two locations in our history. We celebrated our one hundredth anniversary in 1938 and our fiftieth in 1974! Ignorance persists. Can you correctly identify the three most significant statues on campus (two are on East and one is on West)? Do you know why we have a Blue Devil for a mascot? Do you know the words to the alma mater?

How does an institution develop an understanding of its history or appreciation of its past accomplishments? What constitutes pride and loyalty in a university setting among students, faculty, staff, alumni, and friends? Are such intangibles even important or are they vestiges of quaint periods in the past?

Institutional history is imparted in both formal and informal ways. At Duke one can learn from several outstanding historical monographs or from almost daily student-directed campus tours. Since 1972, the official repository for records and information about the university has been the University Archives. Names on quadrangles, gardens, buildings, living groups, seminar rooms, endowments, and awards instruct, as do the selection and display of portraits and statuary. Respect of donor's wishes, physical maintenance of gifts, and attention to detail and accuracy instruct too.

Freshman beanie of Carl H. King, Class of 1924, the last class of Trinity College.

For decades instruction in tradition and history was part of student orientation at Duke. Twin aims were developing class identity and school spirit, particularly in support of athletics. At the turn of the century, entering men are pictured wearing blue and white beanies with a prominent F, like a scarlet letter, on them. This obvious identification gave way to hats with TC for men and women, and then dinks for men and bows for women with specific class designations like 5D4 for the class of 1954. Such labeling explicitly identified first year students so that upperclassmen could ask them to recite cheers, sing the fight song or answer questions about campus lore or history. A written traditions test had to be passed or one had to wear a yellow dink or bow which further increased harassment by upperclassmen. All orientation in school spirit was directed toward the annual Duke-Carolina football game which if Duke won meant that dinks and bows were discarded, but if Duke lost, they had to be worn until the end of the first se-

Freshmen purchasing a new style "dink" in 1950.

mester. Student government appointed a Traditions Board which administered the indoctrination program.

Such archaic practices died a perhaps deserved death in the 1960's when all authority and accepted campus traditions came under close scrutiny. Unfortunately, no program of instruction in history and tradition replaced that of the Traditions Board. Mockery, as in asking how many beer cans tall was the chapel tower, and the proliferation of oral history with consequent inaccuracies and myths became commonplace.

Many individuals have long been concerned over the absence of a coherent plan at the university to impart a sense of history and pride in the institution. In 1993–94, active and engaged alumni, parents, and students, working through the executive committee of the Duke Annual Fund, initiated a program now called "Building Bridges: Creating A Lifelong Commitment to Duke." The centerpiece of the program is a Student Education Initiative formulated by a committee consisting of representatives of class and student government, and the offices of alumni affairs, admissions, student development, annual fund, and the university archives. Embraced by President Keohane and initially coordinated by Sterly Wilder, the Student Education Initiative is a multi-faceted program designed to be carried out in a four-year-cycle and coordinated with the fifth and tenth year class reunions.

Revived past programs and selected traditional programs are designed to be part of a coordinated package. With a new twist of past practice, all first-year students are invited to a social evening at the president's house in a popular staggered event throughout the year called "Desert with the President." The very successful class picnics are enhanced with the holding of the sophomore picnic off campus at the local state historic site, the Duke Homestead, home of philanthropist Washington Duke and birthplace of his children, benefactors Benjamin N. and James B. Duke. The popular first-year picture book continues the glossary of campus language and lore along with an updated historical timeline but an additional page of history has been added. Initially this page explains the origin of the Blue Devil mascot. Each class receives directed mailings which to date have been entitled "Myths Dispelled," "Defining Moments in the History of Duke University," and "The Bean Counters Guide to Finances at Duke" for the first-year, sophomore and junior classes. These brochures are expertly written, attractively designed with numerous illustrations and usually in demand by various campus programs as soon as they appear.

Instruction in campus history is included in a humorous as well as serious look at previous first-year orientation programs through a slide show prepared by the university archivist especially for the first-year orientation staff (FAC) and resident advisors (RA). The show called, "The Tradition Continues," includes historical illustrations from academic, athletic, and student life throughout Duke's history. Among selected mailings all students receive packets of colorful picture post cards

For years the Traditions Board required freshman women to wear bows and men to wear dinks with their class designation on them. If Duke won the Carolina football game their use could be discontinued.

of campus scenes for their own use as well as reminders of special events like Founders' Day. The spring and summer schedule of national alumni events and acceptance parties for newly admitted students, to which all students are invited, is published in the *Chronicle* so students may participate in their hometown or place of summer employment. The renovation of the East Campus Union provided the opportunity for the permanent mounting of eight greatly enlarged photographs of historical scenes in the history of the original Durham campus.

Duke's impressive graduation weekend serves as a perfect transitional point from student to alumnus. In addition to the senior class picnic, alumni affairs hosts the grand graduation party under a massive tent for the graduates and their family and friends. Alumni parents and their graduating sons and daughters get additional attention with a breakfast before commencement exercises welcoming all to the ever expanding family of Duke alumni. For the graduates, attention then shifts to a variety of programs building active involvement and a lifelong commitment for young alumni to their alma mater. Initial focus is on maintaining an up-to-date address for the frequently moving young alumni and their fifth and tenth reunions. The careful planning and implementation of the four-year Student Education Initiative forms a foundation to expand current student interest beyond basketball and bench burning.

Books About Duke:
Eight Variations on a Theme _____

At long last, the first history of Duke as a university has appeared with the release of Robert F. Durden's *The Launching of Duke University, 1924–1949* (Duke Press, 572 pages). This completes a trilogy of books, each very valuable but quite different, about the history of the institution. In 1950 the Duke Press published Nora C. Chaffin's *Trinity College 1839–1892: The Beginnings of Duke University*. Unfortunately out of print, Chaffin's volume remains the only detailed account of the history of the precursor institutions to Duke University before the school moved to Durham. Encyclopedic in nature with a helpful, complete index, the volume recounts the transition from Brown's Schoolhouse to Union Institute in 1839, the brief experiment as Normal College, and the change to Trinity College in 1859 with a successful affiliation with the Methodist Church. It also serves as an excellent representative history of the development of private higher education in the south. Since one man, Braxton Craven, dominated the school in the nineteenth century, Chaffin's account could be considered a biography of one of the country's foremost educators as well.

Earl W. Porter's *Trinity and Duke, 1892–1924* (Duke Press, 1964, 274 pages) recounts the history of the college after it relocated to Durham, but before it became a university. Eminently readable, Porter's account has colorful personalities like President John C. Kilgo, quiet yet no less forceful, significant characters like Washington and Benjamin N. Duke, and dramatic events such as the controversy over academic freedom concerning Professor John Spencer Bassett. It clearly describes the development of Trinity College in Durham into one of the regions strongest liberal arts colleges, worthy of being the foundation of a private research university.

Durden's narrative carries the chronological story from the dramatic turn of events with James B. Duke's unprecedented gift in 1924 to the transition to post-World War II leadership with the selection of A. Hollis Edens as president in 1949. Perhaps this initial volume of the university's history has been a long time coming because of the complexity of the story. With university status one immediately has to deal with the history of a school of religion, graduate school, law school, medical school, and school of forestry as well as the undergraduate school of Trinity College with its engineering, nursing and separate men's and women's components. Author of the acclaimed *The Dukes of Durham, 1865 to 1929* (Duke Press, 1975, 295 pages), Durden is well prepared for the task. He is accomplished in making clear generalizations out of complicated developments and he does not shirk controversy. The reader will discover an obvious hero in President William Preston Few, but Few's trials over developing a proper form of university governance are not glossed over.

Even though Durden's volume is a well-told story, it raises questions as an initial narrative should. The University and the history of higher education ideally would be served if this volume would prompt more detailed accounts of each of Duke's professional and undergraduate schools. Only the medical school has the beginnings of its own history with the publication of James F. Gifford's *The Evolution of a Medical Center: A History of Medicine at Duke University to 1941* (Duke Press, 1972, 249 pages). A variety of additional publications about Duke's long institutional history exists. Too little known but greatly valued volumes are *The Papers and Addresses of William Preston Few* (Duke Press, 1951, 369 pages) by Robert H. Woody, *The Architecture of Duke University* (Duke Press, 1939, 74 pages) by William Blackburn, and *The Library of the Woman's College, Duke University, 1930–1972* (Regulator Press, 1978, 140 pages) by Betty Irene Young. Several undergraduate honors papers in the University Archives also are outstanding additions to the historical record. Durden's history is highly recommended and it should play a vital part in helping the university understand its historical role. It also will be highly successful if it prompts further investigation into a variety of published works or prompts one to add to the record of the rich and varied history of the institution.

Robert F. Durden, Professor of History and Duke family and university historian, conducts a seminar.

Index